TO.
TEXAS WINE....S

An Opinionated Guide for Wine Tourists

By ANDREW CHALK

Great Texas Line Press

Top Texas Wineries
An Opinionated Guide for Wine Tourists

By Andrew Chalk

Editor: Amy Culbertson
Book design: Tom Johanningmeier
Cover design: Jared Stone
Cover photo: Derris Lanier, courtesy of Perissos Vineyards
imagesbyderris.com

Back Cover Photos (from top):
1. Courtesy of Perissos Vineyard, Jeremy Wilson
2. McPherson Cellars, © Laurence Parent
3. Courtesy of Kiepersol Estates
4. McPherson Cellars, © Laurence Parent

© Copyright: MMXIX, Great Texas Line Press
1st edition
10 9 8 7 6 5 4 3 2 1

Bulk sales of books from the Great Texas Line Press are available at special discounts for fundraising, promotions and premiums. For bulk and whole-sale questions, contact:

Great Texas Line Press
Post Office Box 11105
Fort Worth, Texas 76110
817-922-8929 / FAX 817-926-0420
greattexas@hotmail.com / greattexasline.com

Printed in USA

TABLE OF CONTENTS

INTRODUCTION

If you enjoy wine and have a thirst to know more about the Texas wine industry, this book was written for you. According to state figures, there are now almost 500 wineries in Texas, but these numbers are wildly misleading: They include not only producing wineries but also permits that allow direct shipping to consumers, many of which have been obtained by out-of-state shippers. By my estimates, Texas has about 150 wineries that are actually producing. Of that group, about 40 are aspirational, in the sense of trying to make the best wine they can, using Texas grapes. This book winnows out those winners. It gives you an overview of the Texas wine industry, lists my personal selection of the top 40-some and then zooms in on 16 of the very best to visit and buy from. Fortunately, you could not pick a better time to start exploring.

I am a wine writer based in Texas, where I have lived for more than 36 years. My first experiences with Texas wine came on weekend tasting tours with my girlfriend. I began to compare the generally negative aspersions I'd read about Texas wine with the wine I had in my glass. I discovered that I had run into every writer's dream — a large variance between the conventional wisdom and reality. The truth abhors a vacuum, and here was a chance for me to fill it. I wrote about my experiences in numerous publications. That was in 2009. Trends that were incipient then have become a stampede today.

We are at an inflection point in the history of the Texas wine industry. Texas grape growers have planted the largest grape acreage ever and continue to expand. Texas wineries are winning more medals than ever before at the toughest wine competitions in the country. Trade shows of Texas wine in New York City sell out in two hours.

In December 2017, *Bloomberg News* wine critic Elin McCoy singled out the 10 most memorable wines among the thousands from all over the world she had tasted during the year, bottles whose prices ranged through hundreds into thousands of dollars. Among the 10 was a 2014 souzão from Bending Branch Winery in Comfort, Texas.

The fundamental driver in all this is the incontrovertible reality that the quality of Texas wine is higher than ever. The state's top restaurants can now list wines with appellations like Texas High Plains and Texas Hill Country alongside Napa Valley and Sonoma Valley without apology, and to much acclaim.

It wasn't always like this. The Texas wine industry suffered years of bad winemaking (some of which can, in truth, still be found). There were (and still are) people who shipped in bulk wine from California by tanker truck for bottling. We are not profiling them. This book is about what I call the New Texas Wine Industry. That industry is defined by winemakers aspiring to make the best wine they possibly can, not the one their accountant says produces the best numbers. It is defined by winemakers using 100 percent Texas grapes. By growers working with winemakers to contrive parsimonious yields that turn out concentrated, complex fruit. By wineries establishing a bond with their customers that becomes a relationship rather than just a transaction. And by all parties maintaining an outward vision to adopt the best equipment and the best viticultural techniques from around the world. Texas now has about 40 wineries that fit this description, and more are springing up every year.

This state of affairs did not come about due to some deus ex machina. It was the tireless work of grape growers and winemakers over a generation that got the industry where it is today. In this short book I highlight a subset of the very best wineries that are also a great pleasure to visit. These are places where you still get to meet the owners in the tasting room; where you can see the barrels in which the wine ages; where you can join the clubs of the wineries that most impress you to receive special small-production wines at the best prices.

One thing we are constantly reminded of with wine is that the subject never gets boring. Every year brings a new vintage that is not quite like any that preceded it. In Texas, it also brings new wineries and new vineyards. This is boom time for Texas wine.

THE NEW TEXAS
WINE INDUSTRY

In the United States, the three West Coast states of California, Oregon and Washington have emerged as national-quality wine producers. California's reputation is global, and Oregon can make that case too, with Washington not far behind.

Beneath these three is a free-for-all of innominate wineries in states all over the map. Somewhere on the radar, Texas gets a mention. It is astonishing that the state has not managed to successfully publicize its wine industry beyond its borders — an incongruous situation for a state widely regarded as having a big mouth. It seems a good time to take stock of where the Texas wine industry is and of its strengths and weaknesses. Speaking as an "insider," things are really exciting right now for Texas wine.

What is a Texas wine?

A Texas wine is one that has the appellation (place of origin) "Texas" on the front label. Alternatively, it may have a subzone of Texas: for example, the name of a county or an American Viticultural Area within the state. (An American Viticulture Area, or AVA, is a geographically distinct federally designated grape-growing region.) In Texas, eight AVAs have been designated, but the two you are most likely to see on labels are "Texas High Plains" and "Texas Hill Country." If you see an AVA on the front label, 85 percent of the grapes in the wine must come from that AVA. If you see a geographical area, 75 percent of the grapes must come from that geographical area. If you see "Estate-Bottled" on the front label, 100 percent of the grapes must come from vineyards owned or controlled by the producer, and those vineyards must be in an AVA. Thus, we have a hierarchy of quality:

American > Texas > AVA > Estate-Bottled > Texas County

Authenticity

In Texas' relatively young wine industry, the demand for Texas-grown grapes has typically exceeded the amount the state's grape growers have been able to produce. Recent increases in acreage and yields have begun to redress the imbalance, but for years the reputation of the Texas wine industry suffered from the practice of reselling California bulk wine in bottles adorned with Texas symbology to fool consumers into believing that their contents came from Texas.

By printing "For Sale in Texas Only" (FSITO) on the back label (usually in tiny script), the seller was exempted from the federal truth-in-labeling laws, which require the origin of the grapes to appear on the label, and subject only to the far more lenient state law, which does not. Consumers who discovered the deception were likely to stop looking for Texas wines, figuring they could just cut out the middleman and buy California wine directly. That reduced the demand for real Texas wine. It was also inexcusable. There is an honest way to label this bulk wine: Just use the "American" appellation on the front label, and don't use pictures of longhorns, the Texas flag and such.

The recent history of the Texas wine industry is marked by several milestones for authenticity:

• Resentment against the "For Sale in Texas Only" ruse in recent years has led most wine sellers who target the supermarket shelves — with only a few holdouts — to switch to using the

"American" appellation for their non-Texas bottles.

• The Texas Department of Agriculture has a program to promote Texas produce and products called "Go Texan." As the program was initially conceived, a wine carrying the "Go Texan" logo was not required to have a minimum percentage of Texas grapes. The department has since changed its rules to require that, from the 2014 vintage onward, wines labeled "Go Texan" must be from at least 75 percent Texas fruit.

• In early 2017, Rep. Jason Isaac proposed in the Texas House a measure that would raise the required percentage of Texas grapes in a Texas-appelled wine to 100 percent, from the current federal minimum of 75 percent. This move would echo steps taken by the three big West Coast wine-producing states. Among growers, wineries and consumers, there is near-universal agreement that 100 percent is where we need to go. Disagreement on the bill, however, centered on the timetable for its implementation. Many winemakers wanted a five- or 10-year phase-in period to plant vineyards and build up wine inventories against a wipeout harvest. The resolution failed to become law in the 2017 legislative session, but supporters, myself among them, intend to see it introduced in the next legislative session with a generous phase-in period and broad industry support.

• Dallas-based liquor store chain Sigel's announced in March 2017 that it would no longer shelve Texas wines and FSITO wines together and would replace most FSITO wine with Texas equivalents. The change led to a new supply of several Texas wines and should act as a bellwether for other wine stores in the state.

The vineyards

There are around 8,000 acres of wine grapes in Texas. That makes the state the country's fifth-largest in terms of vineyard area, and the acreage is increasing at a strong 10 percent per year.

Although grapes are grown all over the state, 70 percent or more of the vineyard land is in the Texas High Plains AVA (around Lubbock). There, altitudes between 2,900 and 4,100 feet and desert humidity conditions create the 30-degree-plus diurnal shifts of warm days to cool nights and the long hang times required for grapes to achieve full phenolic ripeness, with its attendant mellowing of astringency. The dry climate also is inimical to diseases that commonly plague the vines.

The most famous High Plains vineyard is Neal and Janice Newsom's Newsom Vineyard, near Plains, a short distance from the New Mexico state line. Longtime evangelizers for High Plains viticulture, the Newsoms are universally revered in the Texas wine industry.

There is no practical cap for the future on planted acreage in Texas, as the High Plains has, in the words of consultant Bobby Cox of Pheasant Ridge, "only six million acres." Grapes use only a quarter of the water required by the cotton that vines typically supplant. This gives farmers in the area who have long been dependent on row crops in the face of ongoing groundwater depletion an added incentive to plant some of their acreage in higher-profit-for-acre grapes. The price of land in the High Plains, often less than $2,000 per acre for irrigated land, is lower than that of just about every other grape source in the country as well.

Another viticultural trend making itself seen in Texas is vineyard source diversification. In a state whose area is larger than France, growers can plant vineyards in multiple locations to balance out the effects of frost, hail and disease. Hill Country wineries that hitherto may have relied on grapes from the High Plains are now planting in their own AVA. Wineries north and east of Dallas are planting in Collin and Grayson counties. One grower, Square Cloud Winery in Gunter, cultivates no fewer than 25 grape varieties, a virtual private agricultural experimental station, from which it will eventually winnow out the best.

The grapes

Thirty years ago, grape plantings in Texas consisted of varieties that sold well in the national market. Years of marginal winemaking gave those varieties a reputation for producing poor wine and for "not working" in the Texas climate. Chardonnay, cabernet sauvignon and pinot noir were the three best-known examples. A number of winemakers and grape growers turned to predominantly Mediterranean varieties, expecting that they were better adapted to Texas' hot climate and would "work better" here. Meanwhile, winemaking skills improved as the years went on.

In the last few years the evidence has steadily mounted that the grapes may not have been the whole problem.

First came good Texas chardonnay — both Chablis-style from Inwood Estates Vineyards (grown in Dallas County, would you believe) and lush New-World-style from Fall Creek Vineyards and Arché. Then Pheasant Ridge Winery, Inwood Estates Vineyards, Newsom Vineyards and Calais Winery, among others, proved that good cabernet sauvignon was possible in Texas. The grape that appeared to be truly impossible to conquer in Texas was pinot noir — until very recently: The Bar Z Winery 2016 "Bayer Family Vineyard" pinot noir (tasted in barrel) is a breakthrough wine; Randall Grahm, owner of Bonny Doon Vineyard, called it "delightfully amazing." Zinfandel is the holdout that, so far, remains beyond reach.

Temperate-climate grapes like the above acknowledged, it must be noted how many Mediterranean grapes are thriving in the hot climate of Texas. Among white *Vitis vinifera* (European wine grapes), albariño, muscat, picpoul, roussanne, trebbiano, vermentino and viognier are most widely grown. The list of *vinifera* reds is even longer. Tempranillo is the state's poster child; others include aglianico, montepulciano, mourvèdre, petite sirah, sangiovese, syrah, tannat and touriga nacional.

Even blanc du bois — an American hybrid grape created at the

University of Florida to resist the insect-borne bacteria that causes the deadly Pierce's disease — continues to improve in Texas. It shines in dessert wines inspired by Haak Vineyards & Winery's innovative "Texas Madeira" and as a southern-Rhône-style white wine at Haak and at the Vineyard at Florence. Its future, however, may be as a sparkling wine, given its high acidity. The seeds of a sparkling-wine industry have just germinated in Texas, and it will take years to determine what *cépage* and method work best. My bet is on blanc du bois made in the same style as prosecco and possibly cut with a little viognier.

The people

Winemaker knowhow is increasing rapidly across the state. It has become more and more common for winery owners to employ experienced winemakers from established vineyards in California and other states; in 2013, Fall Creek Vineyards boldly stepped into the global market and hired Chilean Sergio Cuadra, formerly of Concha y Toro and Caliterra, as its chief winemaker.

Academic support for winemaking and viticulture comes from several schools. Texas Tech, long associated with Texas winemaking, offers viticulture programs in Lubbock and Fredericksburg. Texas A&M, the state's primary agricultural research facility, has a minor in viticulture, and Grayson County College, in the northeast of the state, has had a large and underappreciated influence on Texas winemaking with its certificate programs.

Up-and-coming and turnaround wineries

Among established wineries, one of the most striking turnarounds has been at Fall Creek, where Cuadra turns out winner after winner, especially its Certenberg Vineyards chardonnay. Spicewood Vineyards has emerged as a contender recently, with strong expressions of sauvignon blanc and tempranillo. One of the state's largest wineries, Llano Estacado, is making better wine than ever and has invested in a "Napa-quality" visitor center in Lubbock.

In northeast Texas, Arché, situated on a dome above the Red River that defines the terroir of the region, made a roussanne that platinum-medaled (93 points) at the 2014 San Diego International Wine Competition, bringing attention to its consistently strong line of roussanne and chardonnay wines.

The new kid on the block everybody is talking about, Lewis Wines (not to be confused with Napa's Lewis Cellars), offers a tempranillo that exudes winemaking experience far beyond the winery's years. William Chris makes a mourvèdre that is putting the grape on the state's map. The High Plains' Bingham family, long one of the state's largest grape growers but having opened a winery only in the last few years, is already winning numerous medals for its Bingham Family Vineyards wines.

Perhaps the biggest turnaround story (and one that might merit a class project by a business school student aiming to go into winery management) is Messina Hof. Though its owners have been tireless promoters of the Texas wine industry, Messina Hof used to have a lot of FSITO wines in its product range, as though authenticity were an afterthought. Then, in a total change of direction, this 40-year-old winery, one of the largest in the state, executed a shift to 100 percent Texas grapes. From 2015 every wine has been appellated "Texas." This entailed large long-term contracts with growers in the High Plains AVA, a change in varietal mix and lots of explanatory talks with retail partners. The winery is winning more medals than ever. The fact that Messina Hof can make the shift serves as a lesson to other large Texas wineries.

How good is the product?

All the above speaks to the underpinnings of the Texas wine industry, but good wine trumps all else, and Texas will be judged by its output. How do we measure how good the wine is now? The fact is that the best of it is much better than the credit it is given in most of the literature. If you have bad wine on your first try, you will be dissuaded from coming back, as many people from both inside and outside the state have been. What those naysayers have missed in the interim is that the best producers have quietly improved to the point that they can now be served at the same table as wines from anywhere in the country.

There are a number of ways of showing this improved quality. Blind tastings by knowledgeable palates, alongside wines from out-of-state, can be indicative. Another indication of quality may be the most compelling of all: The chart below plots the total number of medals — gold, silver and bronze — won each year at out-of-state wine competitions by Texas wines (those made from at least 75 percent Texas grapes), from 1984 (six medals) on the extreme left to 2017 (162 medals) on the extreme right. More than 80 percent of the medals below were awarded at the San Francisco International Wine Competition, the *San Francisco Chronicle* Wine Competition, the Finger Lakes International Wine Competition, the Los Angeles International Wine Competition and the San Diego International Wine Competition, the most respected national competitions. Two are actually from the Lyon International Wine Competition in France.

With a couple of anomalous spikes, the number of medals awarded each year oscillated around 20 until 2011, when we began to see a significant climb. The next year the number broke 50. Those years marked an inflection point, with the annual medal count showing exponential growth. While the relatively low number of medals in earlier years can be partly attributed to sketchy reporting, the main reason for the increase starting in 2011 is a massive improvement in the quality of the wine. Wineries that would not have considered entering out-of-state competitions several years ago, because of the minuscule prospect of a medal, are now much

Medals won by Texas wineries in out-of-state competitions

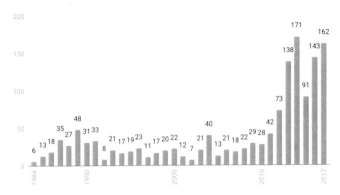

more willing to bear the entry costs.

The recent data show a sharp drop in the number of medals won in 2015. The reason was the disastrous 2013 harvest, a result of the worst weather for Texas grape growers in more than 60 years, depressing the number of competition-worthy wines available in 2015. The figures rebounded with an equally dramatic relative increase in 2016, and in 2017 the numbers continued the general upward trend, approaching the record set three years before in 2014.

The above chart actually understates the number of medals Texas wines win in national competition. That's because it excludes in-state competitions, even though the major Texas competitions judge many more out-of-state wines than Texas wines. The major competitions in Texas are Tarrant County's Lone Star International Wine Competition, the state's oldest wine competition, founded in Grapevine by the Texas Wine and Grape Growers Association; the Houston Livestock Show and Rodeo (officially branded "Rodeo

Uncorked!"); the TEXSOM International Wine Awards in Dallas; and the San Antonio Stock Show & Rodeo Wine Competition. I estimate that Texas wines won at least as many medals at these shows as at the out-of-state shows, so omitting them actually biases the test against Texas wines and therefore strengthens the conclusion about the recent improvement in quality.

Success is a trend

In the Texas wine industry, individually successful efforts — such as Haak's successful adoption of the *estufagem* process, heating wine over time to make a Madeira-like wine — have been noted for many years. What is new these days is a systematic, across-the-board and consistent elevation in the level of quality at wineries, year-in and year-out.

While these improvements are impressive, nobody can rest on his or her laurels. Winemakers and grape growers in Texas, by and large, recognize that they still don't know much about the best places to plant grapes, even as they are getting a better idea of which grapes to plant. The biggest problem, it has been argued, is the need for even more winemaking expertise, and that can come only with time.

TEXAS WINE TOURISM

Wine and tourism invariably have a synergistic relationship, and Texas has been no exception. A study by WineAmerica.org estimated that Texas wineries generated 1.7 million tourist visits and $717 million in spending in 2017.

Awareness of Texas as a wine destination has been slow to emerge nationally, but that appears to be changing. *USA Today's* nationwide 2018 Reader's Choice poll of the country's best tasting rooms placed three wineries from Texas — more than any other state, including California — in its top 10: Bending Branch in Comfort (No. 3), Brennan in Comanche (No. 5) and Spicewood Vineyards (No. 6). Meanwhile, Lonely Planet recently released a handsomely designed hardback guide titled "Wine Trails: United States & Canada" in which two of Texas' wine regions, the High Plains and the Hill Country, are spotlighted.

By far the strongest tourism magnet is the Texas Hill Country, from Tow in the north to the San Antonio exurbs in the south and from I-35 west to Mason. Here, more than 70 wineries are making wine, and virtually all of those have a visitor facility, from "Napa-grade" specially built structures to converted homes and outbuildings. Many have thriving events sidelines, hosting meetings, weddings and other celebrations.

The shop window of the Texas wine industry is the section of U.S. 290 between Johnson City and Fredericksburg, with an ever-growing number of wineries vying for the visitor's attention along its 36-mile length. More recent years have seen winemakers from other parts of the state opening ambitious tasting rooms along 290 to get in on the action on the second-most-traveled wine route in the United States, after Napa's Highway 29.

The tirelessly quaint town of Fredericksburg, having painstakingly preserved its German pioneer buildings and its Victorian charm, has emerged as the de facto core of the visitor end of the Texas wine industry. Wine bars and wine shops are not hard to find, including some with a decidedly Texas bent, and several wineries run tasting rooms in town. There are lots of hotels and B&Bs as well as a growing restaurant scene, including one establishment, the Cabernet Grill, that pioneered the idea of an all-Texas wine list. Main Street is full of idiosyncratic gift and antique shops, and there are everyday necessities in the likes of Walmart and other chain retailers just outside the town's core. Both Austin and San Antonio are less than an hour-and-a-half's drive away. If I were visiting the area for more than a day, I would stay in Fredericksburg and use it as a base to explore some of the more than 50 wineries within a one-hour drive (most of them noted in this book).

Smaller tourist clusters include:

Lubbock: This is the commercial center of the Texas High Plains, the principal grape-growing area in Texas. From here you can visit McPherson Cellars (right in town), Llano Estacado, Pheasant Ridge Winery and Trilogy Cellars, all of which are recommended in this book, as well as CapRock Winery, whose recent retooling with respected High Plains grower Steve Newsom overseeing the wines makes it a player to watch. Within an hour's drive to the south are Bingham Family Vineyards' Meadow Vineyards and Winery, open by appointment, and Texas Custom Wine Works, whose facilities are used by some respected names and whose tasting room showcases the results — including sparkling wine. A little farther afield, to the north toward Amarillo, is Bar Z Winery.

Lubbock has plenty of hotels, on account of the huge Texas Tech campus, and unless a Tech event is going on the hotels are mostly inexpensive. The late rock 'n' roll great Buddy Holly was born here, and there is a museum to commemorate him. The budding nightlife and arts district surrounding it, the Depot District, is home to both McPherson Cellars and McPherson's wife's restaurant and wine bar La Diosa Cellars.

Grapevine: I include this town near the DFW airport solely in order to say "caveat emptor." Despite all its wine-themed trappings, the pervasive reality of Grapevine in terms of the wine produced or sold there is a dearth of quality control. A lot of the wines are actually California jug wine labeled to appear to be Texas wines. Others are kit wines. Of the two satellites of quality wineries in town, Bingham Family Vineyards and Messina Hof Winery, both wineries have tasting rooms at their home bases and in the Hill Country.

Possible future hubs: It will be interesting to see what emerges off the beaten wine-tourism path. On the northern fringes of the Hill Country, Mason County and the appealingly unspoiled town of San Saba are emerging as possible winery centers.

Mason County has Sandstone Cellars and the original Compass Rose production facility in Mason; the nearby Robert Clay Vineyards (whose owner started a viticulture program at Mason High School); Fly Gap Winery in the hamlet of Art; and, in tiny Pontotoc, Pontotoc Vineyard, Dotson & Cervantes and Don Pullum's nascent Akashic Vineyard Winery.

San Saba has Wedding Oak as a solid anchor, along with the Old Man Scary Cellars tasting room and a possible new winery in the works from the nearby Good Vibes Vineyard, plus a little boutique inn in an old bank and a historic hotel under renovation.

Comfort, home to Bending Branch Winery and Newsom Vineyards' tasting room, is a possible hub to the south, between Fredericksburg and San Antonio.

THE BEST WINERIES IN TEXAS

This is a personal selection, subject to change as new wineries appear and establish themselves on the Texas winemaking scene, as existing ones grow and evolve and as others slip back. My list of the best includes 43 wineries from around the state, wineries that:

• Are trying to make the best wines possible rather than making wines with the kind of numbers that accountants like to see.

• Are making wines that can be appellated "Texas," or a subzone thereof; most are using 100 percent Texas grapes.

• Are striving to form an enduring bond with their customers through winemaker and owner appearances in the tasting room, really useful wine clubs and helpful Internet communication (e-mail, website, social media).

• Refuse to sell "For Sale in Texas Only" (FSITO) wines. Very few of the wineries listed below make or sell wines from out-of-state juice, but if they do they label them honestly as "American" and do not try to disguise their out-of-state origins by means of FSITO.

From these 43 wineries that have risen to the top of Texas' wine industry, I chose 16 wineries to spotlight in greater detail. Those winery profiles form the heart of this book. They are all wineries that I have visited many times, whose wines I have tasted many times and thus can testify as to their character and consistent quality. They are destination wineries, worthy on their own of a trip, the wineries to visit if you want to know about and appreciate Texas winemaking. In the end, it is a matter of personal taste, but here are some of the criteria I looked for in making my choices:

- A winery owner who has a distinctive, consistent personal vision and palate that clearly shows in his or her wines, and who has made strides in achieving this vision.

- A winery owner who has a distinctive, consistent philosophy that informs the decisions made in his or her winemaking program, tasting-room aesthetics and policies, pricing and other business decisions.

- A winery that has generated favorable opinions and is held in high respect among wine experts and informed wine consumers. This may include but is not limited to high ratings and medals for distinctive vintages in blind-tasting competitions judged by unbiased experts, as well as industry and public buzz generated through publications, blogs and word of mouth.

- Wines that are rewarding to drink and that compel one to taste them again and again.

- Wines that are furthest along in terms of showing results.

- Innovative winemaking policies and philosophies, whether it be a focus on exploring particular grape varietals, winemaking methods or other ideas and innovations that are pushing the Texas wine industry forward.

Note that hours and other information listed here may vary seasonally and with other changes, so it is always best to call ahead and check when you are planning a visit.

The list

Arché: This North Texas gem (pronounced *ar-khay*) is hidden on a knoll near St. Jo overlooking the Red River but just inside Texas. Arché's chardonnay is exceptional, and its roussanne is also among the best in the state. Arché hosts frequent parties and grill-outs with live music and food, and regulars often drop in to grab a bottle to drink with their Neapolitan-style pizza at Ancient Ovens down the road. *228 Wagner Road, Saint Jo. archewines.com. Contact: 214-536-6330, GoodWines@ ArcheWines.com. Tasting room open noon-6p Thu (happy-hour specials), noon-7p Fri-Sat, noon-5p Sun. Tasting fee. Tours by reservation.*

Barking Rocks Winery: Idiosyncratic second-generation Italian-American Lawrence Tiberia, who goes simply by "Tiberia," has been making wine near the Brazos River southwest of Fort Worth since the early 2000s. He runs the best dog patio in the state and often makes good tempranillos too. *1919 Allen Court, Granbury. barkingrockswine.com. Contact: 817-579-0007, tiberia@barkingrockswine.com. Tasting room open 1-5p Sat; open with live music on the first Friday of every month. Tours by request.*

Bar Z Winery: Situated out in remote Canyon, Texas, a place that makes Lubbock seem like a major metropolis, Bar Z is run by Formula One fanatic Monty Dixon. It's the first winery in Texas to make a good pinot noir, hitherto an impossible grape in Texas. *19290 Farm Road 1541, Canyon. barzwines.com. 806-488-2214. Tasting room open 3-9p Wed-Sun, by reservation Mon-Tue. Tasting fee. Tours by reservation.*

Bending Branch Winery: See Page 34. *142 Lindner Branch Trail, Comfort. bendingbranchwinery.com. Contact: 830-995-2948, bbw@bendingbranchwinery.com. Tasting room open 11a-5p Thu, 11a-6p Fri-Sat, noon-5p Sun. Tours 2p Sat, by appointment Thu-Sun. Tour fee.* **Branch on High:** *704 High St., Comfort. Contact: 830-995-3394. Open 4-8p Thu, noon-8p Fri, 11a-8p Sat, noon-5p Sun.*

Bingham Family Vineyards: Long a major-scale Texas High Plains grape-grower, the Bingham family has turned in recent years to making wine. Results so far are promising. The winery is near Lubbock, and there's a tasting room in Grapevine. *Winery: 645 FM 303, Meadow. bingham.wine. Contact: 806-585-6616, friends@Bingham.wine. Tastings, tours by appointment. Tasting room: 620 S. Main St., Grapevine. Contact: 682-651-8668, Grapevine@Bingham.wine. Hours: noon-8 p Mon-Thu, noon-9p Fri, 11 a.m.-9p Sat, 1-6p Sun. Tasting fee.*

Brennan Vineyards: *See Page 37. 802 S. Austin St., Comanche. brennanvineyards.com. Contact: 325-356-9100, info@brennanvineyards. com. Tasting room hours noon-5p Wed-Thu, noon-6p Fri-Sat. Tasting fee.*

Brushy Creek Vineyards: At this long-established winery north of Fort Worth, owner Les Constable makes a huge range of wine, with each offering expressing the grape's unique character. Brushy Creek's 2015 semillon from Cox Vineyard scored a double gold in the 2016 San Francisco International Wine Competition. There's nothing cookie-cutter about Constable, his winery or his wines. *572 CR 2798, Alvord. brushycreekvineyards.com. Contact: 940-427-4747, brushyck@ wf.net. Tasting room open 10a-6p daily.*

Calais Winery: Frenchman Ben Calais moved to Dallas from Paris to work as a software engineer, but his winemaking hobby soon led him to open a winery in the Deep Ellum district in 2008. His next move was to the Hill Country, where he built a traditional "wine cave" dug into a hill, lined with reclaimed wood. He has steadily built a roster of wines, a winery and a reputation for quality, all from scratch. *8115 U.S. 290 West, Hye. calaiswinery.com. Contact: 830-213-2124, info@ calaiswinery.com. Tastings by appointment only, 2-4p Fri, 11a-5p Sat, Sun. noon-4p Sun. Tasting fee.*

Caney Creek Vineyards: Small but growing winery tucked away about halfway between Dallas and Houston in the East Texas town of Grapeland. *7495 CR 2120, Grapeland. Contact: 936-545-3920. By appointment only.*

Compass Rose Cellars: Hye's a Hill Country town whose name is being heard more frequently in conversations about Texas wine. Just off U.S. 290, Compass Rose makes wine that has had some ups and downs but at its best is quite rewarding. There's a tasting room in Fredericksburg too. *compassrosecellars.com. Contact: 830-868-7799, info@compassrosecellars.com.* **Hye:** *1197 Hye-Albert Road. Tasting room open 11a-6p Fri-Sat, noon-5p Sun, by appointment Mon-Thu.* **Fredericksburg:** *401 E. Main St., Suite E1. 2-8p Fri-Sat, noon-5p Sun.*

Duchman Family Winery: *See Page 41. 13308 Farm-to-Market Road 150 W., Driftwood. duchmanwinery.com, Contact: 512-858-1470, info@duchmanwines.com. Tasting room open noon-6p Mon, 11a-8p Tue-Thu, 11a-9p Fri-Sat, 11a-8p Sun. Tasting fee.*

Eden Hill Vineyard: Forty minutes north of Dallas, Eden Hill is making better and better wines each year — in particular, its aglianico, roussanne and marsanne. Very much a family operation — on a working farm where you can also buy fresh eggs — and a winery to watch. *4910 Eden Hill Lane, Celina. edenhill.com. Contact: 214-850-4081, Linda@edenhill.com. Tasting room open 1-6p Thu-Sun. Tours by appointment.*

Fall Creek Vineyards: *See Page 45.* **Tow:** *1820 CR 222. fcv.com. Contact: 325-379-5361, towinfo@fcv.com. Tasting hall open 11a-5p Mon-Sat, noon-4p Sun. Tasting fee. Tours and large-group tastings by appointment.* **Driftwood:** *18059-A FM 1826. fcv.com Contact: 512-858-4050, driftwoodinfo@fcv.com. Tasting room open 11a-7p Mon-Sat, noon-5p Sun.*

Flat Creek Estate: There are plenty of reasons to make your way over the winding roads from Marble Falls to this handsome winery: the Hill Country views, lunch or dinner at the Bistro, a disc golf course, events from star-gazing to cigar-rolling and even the prospect of an overnight stay in the Vintner's Quarters. And, of course, the wines. Check out the "Super Texan" for a solid red. Owners Rick and Madelyn Naber also run a wine bar in Marble Falls, Flat Creek Enoteca. *24912 Singleton Bend E., Marble Falls. flatcreekestate.com. Contact: 512-267-6310. 11a-5p Tue-Sun. Tasting fee; tours and packages by appointment.*

Haak Vineyards & Winery: *See Page 49. 6310 Avenue T, Santa Fe. haakwine.com. Contact: 409-925-1401. Tasting room open 11a-5p Mon-Wed, 11a-6p Thu-Sat, noon-5:30p Sun. Tours Fri-Sun, fee includes tasting; call to confirm availability.*

Hilmy Cellars: *See Page 55. 12346 E. U.S. 290, Fredericksburg. hilmywine.com. Contact: 830-644-2482, info@hilmywine.com Tasting room open 11a-6p Mon-Sat, noon-6p Sun.*

Hye Meadow Winery: Meeting Mike and Denise Batek, founders and owners of this winery in Hye, is like a trip back to hippie life. The wines, however, are quite serious: good and getting better. *10257 US 290, Hye. hyemeadow.com. Contact: 855-493-9463, info@HyeMeadow.com. Tasting room open 11a-5p Mon and Wed-Thu, 11a-6p Fri-Sat, noon-5p Sun. Tasting fee, waived with three-bottle purchase. Tours 11a and 3p Fri-Sat, 3p Sun or by appointment; fee.*

Inwood Estates Vineyards: *See Page 58.* **Dallas:** *1350 Manufacturing St., Suite 209. inwoodwines.com Contact: 214-902-9452, getinfo@inwoodwines.com. Tasting room open 4-6p Fri (call to confirm), noon-5p Sat.* **Fredericksburg:** *10303 U.S. 290, Fredericksburg. inwoodwines.com Contact: 830-997-2304, InwoodFBG@gmail.com. Tasting room open 11a-5p Sun-Thu, 11a-6p Fri.-Sat. Tasting fee.*

Kiepersol Estates: *See Page 64. 3933 FM 344 E., Tyler. kiepersol.com. Contact: 903-894-8995, winery@kiepersol.com. Tasting room open 11a-7p. Guided public tours of winery and distillery at 2 and 4p Sat; guided winery tours 1p Tue-Fri (fee).*

Kuhlman Cellars: Relatively new but promising Hill Country winery that is very well funded. At the tasting room, reserve one of the wine-and-food pairing classes. The "Signature" pairing includes commentary about food-and-wine chemistry by a sommelier. You must book ahead to reserve a tasting (you can do it online). *18421 E. U.S. 290, Stonewall. kuhlmancellars.com. Contact: 512-920-2675, info@kuhlmancellars.com. Tastings by appointment 11a-6p Thu-Sat, noon-5p Mon. Tasting fee.*

Lewis Wines: *See Page 69. 3209 U.S. 290, Johnson City. lewiswines. com. Contact: 512-987-0660, kyle@lewiswines.com. Tasting room open 10:30a-5p daily; reservations recommended; tasting fee refunded with two-bottle purchase. Tours 10a Sat.*

Llano Estacado: *See Page 73. llanowine.com. Contact: 800-634-3854, info@llanowine.com. Tasting room open noon-6p Tue-Fri, 1-5p Sat-Sun. Tours every half-hour; last tour at 4p.*

Los Pinos Ranch Vineyards: East Texas winery with steadily improving quality. Los Pinos keeps a chef on staff, turning out a menu of casual bites. Weekend nights at the tasting room bring an interesting entertainment schedule, too. *658 CR 1334, Pittsburg. lospinosranchvineyards.com. Contact: 903-855-1769, info@LosPinosRanchVineyards. com. Tasting room open 5-9p Thu, noon-11p Fri-Sat, noon-9p Sun. Tours by appointment.*

Lost Draw Cellars: Respected High Plains grower Andy Timmons' diversification into winemaking hit the ground running with medals from the *San Francisco Chronicle* Wine Competition, thanks to his decision to contract with Kim McPherson to make his first wines. His tasting room is just off Texas 16 in Fredericksburg. *113 E. Park St., Fredericksburg. lostdrawcellars.com. 830-992-3251. Email: andrew@ lostdrawcellars.com. Tasting room open noon-5p Mon-Wed, 11a-6p Thu-Sat, noon-5p Sun. Tasting fee.*

Lost Oak Winery: This is a delightful tasting room within easy driving distance of Fort Worth. Lost Oak maintains a busy schedule of live music, fitness and cooking classes, holiday parties and other promotions. You can hike or bike the wooded nature trails; bring your own vittles or purchase one of the winery's picnic totes. Good viognier. *8101 CR 802, Burleson. lostoakwinery.com. Contact: 817-426-6625, info@lostoakwinery.com. Tasting room open noon-8p Wed and Sun, noon-9p Thu-Sat. Tasting fee. Tours by appointment online.*

Majek Vineyard & Winery: The Majeks celebrate their Czech roots at this young Texas winery to keep an eye on. A good stop between San Antonio and Houston near the intersection of I-10 and U.S. 77. *12508 FM 957, Schulenburg. majekvineyard.com. Contact: 210-413-8912, lynne@majekvineyard.com. Tasting room open 4-7p Fri, noon-6p Sat-Sun.*

McPherson Cellars: *See Page 78. 1615 Texas Ave., Lubbock. mcphersoncellars.com. Contact: 806-687-9463, info@mcphersoncellars.com. Tastings and tours: 11a-6p Mon-Sat (reservations required for six or more).*

Messina Hof Winery & Resort: You might call Vincent Bonarrigo the Walt Disney of the Texas wine industry. At their original winery in Bryan, he and his wife Merrill were among the first Texans to build a winery designed as a tourist destination — a veritable wine theme park with a restaurant, a B&B, a lakeside guest center and rose garden on 100 acres. Since then, the family has exported the formula to splashy tasting rooms in Fredericksburg and Bryan, and the second generation has come on board. Though highly visible promoters of the Texas wine industry for some four decades, and quite successful on the competition circuit, the Bonarrigos did not always use Texas grapes. That has all changed, though, and a new emphasis on using only Texas grapes means every Messina Hof wine is now appellated "Texas." messinahof.com. **Bryan:** *4545 Old Reliance Road. Contact: 979-778-9463 or 800-736-9463, marketing@messinahof.com. Tasting room open 10a-7p Mon-Thu, 10a-8p Fri-Sat, 11a-6p Sun (tasting fee; tours with fee).* **Fredericksburg:** *9996 U.S. 290 E. Contact: 830-990-4653, hillcountry@messinahof.com. Tasting room open 11a-6p Mon-Wed, 11a-7p Thu-Fri. 10a-7p Sat, 11a-6p Sun (tasting fee; tour fee, reservations recommended for tours).* **Grapevine:** *201 S. Main St. Contact: 817-442-8463, grapevine@messinahof.com. Tasting room open noon-8p Sun-Tue, to 9p Wed-Thu, to 11p Fri-Sat (tasting free; tours by appointment).*

Pedernales Cellars: *See Page 82. 2916 Upper Albert Road, Stonewall. pedernalescellars.com. Contact: 830-644-2037, tastingroom@pedernalescellars.com. Estate tasting room open 10a-5p Mon-Thu, to 6p Fri-Sat, noon-5p Sun; reservations requested Sat and for groups of more than six.* **Main Street Tasting Room**, *134 E. Main St., Fredericksburg, 11a-6p daily; reservations requested for groups of more than six. Tasting fee; various levels of tastings available by appointment; tours by appointment.*

Perissos Vineyard and Winery: *See Page 86. 7214 Park Road 4 W., Burnet. perissosvineyards.com. Contact: 512-820-2950, Laura@PerissosVineyards.com. Tasting room open noon-5p Thu-Sun. Tasting fee, waived with three-bottle purchase. Tours by appointment.*

Pheasant Ridge Winery: This is a revival of the original flagship of the 1980s, back under its original owner, the pioneering Bobby Cox. Cox planted the first vineyard here in 1978 and casts a long shadow over the Texas wine industry. With him back at the helm, this High Plains winery off the beaten path north of Lubbock is one to watch; Cox's dry chenin blancs and cabernets have attracted particular attention of late. *3507 E. CR 5700, Lubbock. pheasantridgewinery.com. Contact: 806-746-6033, billgipson@aol.com. Tasting room hours 3-8p Fri, noon-7p Sat-Sun. Tasting fee.*

Pontotoc Vineyard: The Pontotoc Weingarten in Fredericksburg, open on weekends, is the most accessible place to taste Pontotoc's solid tempranillos. The winery and Weinhalle, housed in old buildings in the lost-in-time northern Hill Country town of Pontotoc in Mason County, are open only for special events and by appointment. The Money family, which owns the winery, employs the highly respected Don Pullum as head winemaker. ***Fredericksburg:** 320 W. Main St., Fredericksburg. pontotocvineyard.com. Contact: 512-658-0023, info@pontotocvineyard.com. Tasting room open noon-8p Fri-Sat, noon-5p Sun.*

Rancho Loma Vineyards: This venture helmed by Rancho Loma B&B and restaurant owners Robert and Laurie Williamson in Coleman, south of Abilene, has some serious talent aboard and bears close watching. Ed Hellmann, professor of viticulture and enology at Texas Tech, is director of viticulture. Coleman is becoming a bit of an unlikely destination, with the Williamsons' hip Rancho Pizzeria turning out artisanal pies; a treasure trove of mid-century loot at the Bonneville vintage shop; a mid-century-themed B&B, the Terrace Inn; and a restored motor court, Harbord Kourt. *411 S. Commercial Ave., Coleman. rlv.wine/. Contact: 325-625-1010, molly@rlv.wine. Tasting room open 5-9p Thu, noon-10p Fri-Sat, 1-5p Sun. Tasting fee.*

Red Caboose Winery: South of Glen Rose, this Meridian-based winery is turning out some good reds. It also runs a tasting room and deli in the nearby town of Clifton. ***Meridian:** 1147 CR 1110, redcaboosewinery.com. Contact: 254-435-9911, garyredcabooose@hotmail.com. Tasting room open 10a-6p Sat. Tasting fee. **Clifton:** 903 S. Ave. G. 254-675-0099. 1-8p Thu-Fri, 1-9p Sat, 1-5p Sun. Tasting fee.*

Ron Yates Winery: *See Page 90. 6676 U.S. 290 W., Hye. ronyateswines. com. Contact: 512-585-3972, info@ronyateswines.com. Tasting room open 11a-6p daily.*

Sandstone Cellars Winery: Up on the northern fringes of the Hill Country in Mason and very low-key, this winery is easy to overlook but makes good touriga nacionale, thanks to winemaker Don Pullum (see Pontotoc above) and owners Scott Haupert and Manny Silerio. The winery and its adjacent wine bar double as an art gallery, and the front porch makes a fine spot to linger. *211 San Antonio St., Mason. sandstonecellarswinery.com. Contact: 325-347-9463, wine@sandstonecellarswinery.com. 11a-11p Fri-Sat, 11a-2p Sun.*

Solaro Estate: Well-funded producer of quality wines, especially sangiovese. The original Dripping Springs winery is a half-hour west of Austin, set in a curve of Barton Creek, with estate vineyards on property the owners' family, of Italian heritage, has cultivated since 1909. Solaro has also opened an urban winery in Houston. solaroestate. com. **Dripping Springs:** *13111 Silver Creek Road, Dripping Springs. Contact: 832-660-8642, info@solaroestate.com. Tasting room open 11a-5p Sun-Thu, to 7p Fri-Sat. Tasting fee; reserve tasting by reservation. Vineyard and winery tours by appointment. **The Solaro Winery Houston:** 330 T. C. Jester Blvd. Contact: 832-486-7112, info@solaroestate.com. Tasting room open 4-7p Mon-Thu, to 10p Fri, noon-10p Sat. Tasting fee. Tours by appointment.*

Spicewood Vineyards: The wines here just get better and better. Owner Ron Yates bought the winery and vineyards 35 miles northwest of Austin in 2007 from Ed and Madeleine Manigold, who had been making wine since 1992. Yates has a passion for Spanish wines, and Spicewood's Hill Country tempranillo is one of the best. *USA Today* readers gave Spicewood's tasting room the No. 6 spot in the nation in the paper's 2018 Best Tasting Rooms poll. Schedule a tour to check out the underground barrel room. *1419 Burnet County Road 409, Spicewood. spicewoodvineyards.com. Contact: 830-693-5328, wines@spicewoodvineyards.com. Tasting room open 10a-6p Wed-Sat, noon-5p Sun, by appointment Mon-Tue.*

Stone House Vineyard: Shaded by majestic sycamores and flanked by tall Mediterranean cypresses, Stone House, overlooking Lake Travis, is one of the most beautiful wineries to visit in Texas. Native Australian Angela Moench makes the wine, with help from her husband Howard and an Australian assistant winemaker. The estate vineyards produce the best Norton wine I have tasted. *24350 Haynie Flat Road, Spicewood. stonehousevineyard.com Contact: 512-264-3630, info@ stonehousevineyard.com, Tasting room open noon-5p Thu-Sun and by appointment; various levels of tastings with fees; reservations for groups advised. No tours.*

Trilogy Cellars: Formed by three families of growers in the High Plains and now wholly owned by co-founders Chace and Elizabeth Hill, this recent entry into the Texas wine industry has been a breath of fresh air. Trilogy is now the sister winery to the Hills' new Burklee Hill Vineyards. An old building on the square in Levelland houses Trilogy's tasting room, and the Hills are building a Burklee Hill tasting room in Lubbock to showcase wines from both operations. *618 Ave. H, Levelland. trilogycellars.com. Contact: 806-568-9463, info@trilogycellars. com. Tasting room open noon-7p Tue-Wed, noon-8p Thu, noon-10p Fri-Sat, 1-5p Sun.*

Wedding Oak Winery: *See Page 94. weddingoakwinery.com.* **San Saba:** *316 E. Wallace St. Contact: 325-372-4050, info@weddingoak-winery.com. Tasting room open 11a-6p Mon-Thu, 10a-6p Fri-Sat, 11a-5p Sun.* **Wedding Oak Winery Burnet** *(opening spring 2019): 229 S. Pierce St., Burnet.*

Westcave Cellars Winery: As a grower, Allan Fetty supplied grapes to some of the best names in Texas winemaking for years. Now he has introduced his own label, and his wines are showing promise at his winery near the Pedernales River northwest of Austin. *25711 Hamilton Pool Road, Round Mountain. westcavecellars.com. Contact: 512-431-1403, info@westcavecellars.com. Tasting room open by appointment Tue-Thu, 11a-6p Mon and Fri-Sat, noon-6p Sun. Tasting fee. Tours by reservation for groups of four or more.*

William Chris Vineyards: *See Page 100. 10352 U.S. 290, Hye. williamchriswines.com. Contact: 830-998-7654, info@williamchriswines.com. Tasting room open 10a-5p Mon-Wed, 10a-6p Thu-Sat, noon-5p Sun. Tasting fee; reservations recommended Mon-Thu, required Fri-Sun.*

WINERY PROFILES:
THE BEST OF THE BEST

From our selection of wineries producing the best Texas wine, we've highlighted the top destinations we consider the best to visit.

Andrew Chalk

Dr. Robert Young, whose career in medicine inclines him toward the scientific method in winemaking, checks wine aging in barrel at Bending Branch.

BENDING BRANCH WINERY

142 Lindner Branch Trail, Comfort. bendingbranchwinery.com. Contact: 830-995-2948, bbw@bendingbranchwinery.com. Tasting room open 11a-5p Thu, 11a-6p Fri-Sat, noon-5p Sun. Tours 2p Sat, by appointment Thu-Sun. Tour fee. **Branch on High:** 704 High St., Comfort. Contact: 830-995-3394. Open 4-8p Thu, noon-8p Fri, 11a-8p Sat, noon-5p Sun.

Andrew Chalk

A selection of medal-winning Bending Branch wines.

Overview

Head down to Comfort in the south of the Hill Country, and just a couple of miles outside town, on a rolling south-facing hill, you will come across Bending Branch Winery. The tasting room faces the road, with a patio that is popular in the summer. The winemaking takes place in corrugated buildings on the far side of the vineyard.

The winery was founded by Dr. Robert Young and John Rivenburgh in 2009; in 2016 Rivenburgh left to form his own winery and do consulting. Young continues as owner and winemaker, while Jennifer McInnis Fadel is general manager and handles the business side.

A browse through the wines offered on the Bending Branch website might leave you puzzled whether this winery is actually producing Texas wine. A lot of the wines have California appellations like Paso Robles, Sierra Foothills, Alta Mesa. The answer is that Bending Branch has a winemaking facility in California. But there is exemplary Texas wine made here, with grapes from 10 vineyards — three in the Texas Hill Country and seven in the Texas High Plains.

Philosophy

Dr. Young has, as you might expect for a medical doctor, his eye firmly on the scientific method. He has been a leader in introducing to the state two notable techniques from France, cryomaceration (freezing the grapes before fermentation) and flash détente (a process of rapid heating and cooling), designed to extract more flavor and color from grapes.

Significant accomplishments

One of the most remarkable things about Bending Branch is how quickly it has risen into the top rank of Texas wineries. Since its 2009 founding, the winery regularly has won medals at the San Francisco International Wine Competition, one of the most competitive international shows held in the United States, and in 2017 won top Texas red wine at the San Antonio Stock Show & Rodeo Wine Competition for its 2014 Newsom Vineyards Tempranillo (made with 60 percent cryomaceration).

Bending Branch has snagged "Top Texas Winery" titles in two recent awards programs — the 2018 Houston Stock Show & International Wine Competition and the *San Antonio Express-News* 2017 Top 100 dining and beverage rankings. *Express-News* readers also voted it best Texas winery for four consecutive years in the paper's Readers' Choice Awards. And in *USA Today*'s nationwide 2018 reader poll, Bending Branch was voted the third-favorite tasting room in the entire country.

Perhaps the most extraordinary accolade: *Bloomberg News* wine critic Elin McCoy included the 2014 Bending Branch Winery Estate Souzão as one of the most memorable wines she tasted in 2017, calling it "my most surprising wine of the year." It was the first time a Texas wine has been included on such an exalted list.

Best wines

Tannat (one of the winery's signature grapes), tempranillo and the aforementioned souzão (a Portuguese grape) stand out among the reds. The latter grape is something of a personal favorite for Bob Young, and he readily talks about the bright future he thinks it has in Texas. Among the whites, roussanne and picpoul blanc excel.

Visitor tips

Check out nearby Comfort for some antiquing and boutiquing; it's a bit like Fredericksburg back before the tourist buses. Bending Branch also maintains a cutesy-cozy-quaint tasting room and wine bar that's open Thursdays-Sundays on downtown Comfort's High Street, offering Bending Branch and other wines, snacks and desserts; locals know about the Thursday night potlucks there.

BRENNAN VINEYARDS

802 S. Austin St., Comanche. brennanvineyards.com. Contact: 325-356-9100, info@brennanvineyards.com. Tasting room hours noon-5p Wed-Thu, noon-6p Fri-Sat. Tasting fee.

Brennan Vineyards

Brennan Vineyards' tasting room is housed in a historic home built in Comanche in 1876.

Overview

You might not expect wine, really good wine, to come out of Comanche, Texas, but you would be wrong. Two hours southwest of

Brennan's Miguel Suaste with harvested grapes.

Fort Worth is Brennan Vineyards, maker of some of the best-crafted wines in the state.

The centerpiece of the grounds is a historic home known as the McCrary House, constructed in 1876 near Indian Creek, a few blocks from the town square, from 21-inch-thick limestone. Dr. Pat and Trellise Brennan bought it as a getaway in 2000; two years later, having retired and bought 30 acres surrounding their historic cottage, they began planting their Comanche estate vineyard.

Originally they provided grapes for the well-established Becker Vineyards, owned by their friend and colleague Dr. Richard Becker. But Brennan caught the wine bug in earnest and in 2004 began building a winery and first-class tasting room. As the winery grew, he added the Austin House, an expansive events center.

It did not take long for Brennan Vineyards to begin winning

medals at wine shows. In 2007 the Houston Livestock Show and Rodeo International Wine Competition judges named its 2006 Comanche County viognier Top Texas Wine. By 2017, Brennan had brought home a Best of Class award from the *San Francisco Chronicle* Wine Competition for its 2015 reserve viognier and a gold for the 2015 roussanne.

Over less than two decades, the Brennans have built their original garage operation into an impressive wine compound in this west central Texas town of about 4500 souls. Their vineyards supply grapes not only for Brennan wines but for some of Texas' other respected wineries. Like many other top wineries around the state, the Brennans also source grapes for their wines from several Texas High Plains growers.

In 2007 Todd Webster came on board as a winemaking apprentice; today, with enology and viticulture studies at Texas Tech University and Washington State University under his belt, he is the winemaker at Brennan. Particularly notable are his viognier sourced from the estate, as well as his roussanne, nero d'avola (a Sicilian red grape) and tempranillo.

Philosophy

Winemaker Webster subscribes to a minimal-intervention philosophy. He avoids going overboard in pursuit of any one characteristic in his wines, which makes them pair harmoniously with a wide variety of foods.

Significant accomplishments

Pat Brennan has been a tireless advocate for Texas wines of quality, both as a founder of the Texas Fine Wine group, a coalition of five respected wineries, and as a mentor, consultant and speaker.

Brennan collaborated with two other quality-focused wineries, Lost Oak Winery and McPherson Cellars, to form 4.0 Cellars. Their high-visibility, high-design winery is essentially a shared visitor center at a key location on U.S. 290 10 miles east of Fredericksburg. Being at the center of the most popular Texas wine route introduces Brennan wines to many more visitors than his winery would see in Comanche.

Still, the original tasting room has plenty of fans — enough, in fact, to vote it the United States' fifth-best tasting room in *USA Today*'s 2018 top-10 reader poll.

Best wines

Among the whites, I recommend all the viognier and the roussanne. My favorite Brennan red is the tempranillo, and the nero d'avola is worthy as well.

Visitor tips

Brennan's most recent addition is a barrel-room private tasting area in the basement of the event center, where limited-seating reserve tastings are held.

The hardwood-shaded old McCrary homestead is a good starting point for exploring Comanche, a town steeped in frontier history, starting with its namesake tribe. A group of historical markers on the courthouse square includes one commemorating an 1861 Indian raid. Walk north from the winery several blocks on Austin Street to Grand Avenue and you'll find the site of the 1874 shooting of a deputy sheriff by John Wesley Hardin; farther north off Austin Street is a marker commemorating the Hanging Oak, where a mob hanged three of Hardin's relatives for the shooting (Hardin himself had escaped). Their stories and more are told at the Comanche Historical Museum, comanchecountytxmuseum.com.

DUCHMAN FAMILY WINERY

13308 Farm-to-Market Road 150 W., Driftwood. duchmanwinery.com. Contact: 512-858-1470, info@duchmanwines.com. Tasting room open noon-6p Mon, 11a-8p Tue-Thu, 11a-9p Fri-Sat, 11a-8p Sun. Tasting fee.

Duchman Family Winery

The vine-draped Duchman Family Winery presents an imposing presence near Driftwood.

Overview

Duchman Family Winery

Duchman winemaker Dave Reilly.

Duchman Family Winery is situated in the "near east" sector of the Hill Country just 40 minutes from downtown Austin. The driveway winds through the beautiful vineyards, leading you to an elegant Italianate building housing the Italian restaurant Trattoria Lisina on the left and Duchman's imposing vine-draped winery and tasting room on the right.

These were all part of the same operation when they opened in 2004. Restaurateur Damian Mandola, founder of the Carrabba's Italian chain, and Stanley and Lisa Duchman were the owners; the winery was called Mandola Estate Winery; and "Lisina" was a conjunction of Lisa Duchman's and Damian's wife Trina's names. The focus was on Italian grapes.

In 2010, however, the partnership ended, with Mandola keeping the restaurant and Duchman the winery. There was extensive litigation involved, and this left some bad blood: Damian Mandola was arrested twice at the winery in April 2014, on charges of burglary, assault with a deadly weapon and criminal mischief on the winery premises. Two felony charges were eventually dismissed, but as of press time in late 2018 Mandola still faced a misdemeanor and a felony charge arising from the two incidents.

Despite these incidents, the winery continues to thrive. The Duchmans have shown an uncanny ability to surround themselves with quality people. Their initial viticultural consultant was Bobby Cox, who had made wines praised by the world's most influential wine critic, Robert Parker, at Pheasant Ridge Winery. The respected Mark Penna was the first head of vineyard operations and wine-maker. Tragically, Penna died in 2011 after a three-year battle with brain cancer. The winery saw a smooth succession, however, as Penna's assistant of three years, Dave Reilly, took over.

Under both winemakers, the wines of Duchman Family Winery have consistently won medals. All Duchman grapes are Texas-grown; there are 20 vineyard acres on the Driftwood property, but the bulk comes from the Texas High Plains.

Philosophy

"100 percent Texas grapes, 100 percent Texas wine" is what it says on the home page of the Duchman website, and that pretty much sums up most of the philosophy that guides the winery.

In addition to its commitment to authenticity, the winery is also committed to quality and reasonable prices. Those things, and good sales management by Jeff Ogle, have made Duchman wines one of the most widely distributed Texas portfolios in restaurants and retail stores across the state.

Significant accomplishments

Duchman was the first Texas winery to "keg" wines, packaging it in pressurized reusable plastic barrels for serving in bars and restaurants. The advantages are lower packaging costs and less waste and breakage. With kegging volume growing at 10 percent a year, Duchman kegs its trebbiano, vermentino, montepulciano and its Grape Growers Blend to great commercial success and no loss of quality.

Best wines

Personal favorites among the whites are the trebbiano and vermentino; among the reds, I like the sangiovese, montepulciano and aglianico.

Stan and Lisa Duchman with winemaker Dave Reilly, right.

Visitor tips

You can bring a picnic and linger at the tables under the oaks on the Duchman grounds, but most visitors pair a tasting at the winery with a meal on the neighboring Mandola Estate at Trattoria Lisina. With lushly planted gardens, a massive arched entrance and imposing dining rooms, Trattoria Lisina offers upscale Italian fare and fancy pizzas (reservations recommended).

The high quality of Duchman's wines combined with the promise of a leisurely meal and a view of the cypress-studded Tuscan-esque grounds make Duchman and its neighbor among the most-visited destinations in this part of the Hill Country, even though, not surprisingly, neither establishment is mentioned on the other's website.

FALL CREEK VINEYARDS

Tow: 1820 CR 222. fcv.com. Contact: 325-379-5361, towinfo@fcv. com. Tasting hall open 11a-5p Mon-Sat, noon-4p Sun. Tasting fee. Tours and large-group tastings by appointment. **Driftwood:** 18059-A FM 1826. fcv.com. Contact: 512-858-4050, driftwoodinfo@fcv.com. Tasting room open 11a-7p Mon-Sat, noon-5p Sun.

Fall Creek Vineyards

Fall Creek Vineyards overlooks Lake Buchanan.

Overview

A trip to France in 1973 to look for breeding cattle for their ranch changed the lives of Ed and Susan Auler forever. They went over as ranchers and came back as incipient winemakers. By 1975 Ed had a test plot of *vinifera* vines in a corner of his Fall Creek ranch in Tow on the west bank of Lake Buchanan, a vast artificial lake created in the late 1930s to supply water, power and recreational opportunities to the area. That quarter-acre made great wine.

By 1979 the Aulers' vineyards had grown to 7½ acres, and Auler decided to give up his law practice to make wine full-time. During the 1980s, the Aulers brought in noted enologist André Tchelist-cheff, who was instrumental in the evolution of California winemaking, to consult on the planting of *vinifera* cabernet sauvignon vines. Eventually, Fall Creek Vineyards acquired 400 acres, and the winery and visitors' facilities, felicitously situated overlooking Lake Buchanan, expanded as well.

In 2013, at the recommendation of California winemaker Paul Hobbs, the Aulers hired Sergio Cuadra from Chile's Concha y Toro, the dominant Latin American producer and a major global player. In 2016, Cuadra in turn hired Phil Price away from BRAND Napa Valley, where he had worked as winemaker with Philippe Melka.

In 2015 the Aulers opened Fall Creek Vineyards at Driftwood, a smaller winery and vineyard at a picturesque corner opposite the famous Salt Lick BBQ. Producing grenache, syrah, mourvèdre, tempranillo and sangiovese grapes, the Salt Lick vineyard is one of several named Texas vineyards from which the winery has developed its portfolio of offerings.

Philosophy

Fall Creek has built its empire on Hill-Country-grown Texas grapes and an aspiration to make the best wine possible. Commendably, even its separate "Classics" tier of cash-flow supermarket wines boasts 100 percent Texas-grown grapes.

Significant accomplishments

The Aulers were the first to grow grapes and make wine commercially in the Texas Hill Country. Their winery served as something of a template for many of those that followed, and they have been tireless promoters of the Hill Country as a wine region. In 1986 the Aulers founded the Texas Hill Country Wine & Food Festival.

Drawing on his professional legal training, Ed Auler was the petitioner for the establishment of the Texas Hill Country American Viticultural Area, Texas' second AVA, which the federal government granted in 1990.

The Aulers signaled the seriousness of their commitment to quality when they stepped into the global marketplace to lure Cuadra away from Concha y Toro, a real coup for a Texas winery. As director of winemaking, Cuadra has elevated the quality of Fall Creek wines, leading to a precipitous increase in recognition through medals at national wine competitions.

Best wines

Meritus: This Bordeaux blend is Fall Creek's *tête de cuvée.* When people maintain that cabernet sauvignon does not work in Texas, this is one of the wines you give them to dissuade them of the notion. A complex blend of cabernet sauvignon and merlot, it pairs admirably with red meat.

Chardonnay, Certenberg Vineyard: Proof that chardonnay can be successfully grown in Texas, this is made in a lush, oaky, creamy style. Full malolactic fermentation; barrel-fermented; aged 16 months in new French oak barrels.

GSM: This grenache-syrah-mourvèdre blend has emerged over the past few years as a significant example of its type; great to blind-taste alongside Australian and California examples.

Sauvignon blanc: Sergio Cuadra's first leaf-to-bottle wine in Texas was this wine. I tasted it at Savor Dallas in 2015 and realized immediately that we had a prodigious winemaking talent in the state. It appears to represent a style that is not French nor Californian (and certainly not New Zealand) but somewhere in between, with a more viscous mouthfeel than a Loire wine but less up-front fruit than a California sauvignon blanc.

Visitor tips

For tastings at Tow, it wouldn't hurt to make an advance reservation even if you aren't part of a large group. Fall Creek is the daddy of Hill Country wine tourism and draws plenty of visitors, especially on weekends — though it is, unlike many Texas wineries, open seven days a week.

At the big original tasting room and grounds at Tow, with its graceful allée approach through the vineyards, and in Driftwood's more intimate setting with its cozy-cottage charm, Fall Creek maintains a lively schedule of festivals, special dinners, chef appearances, themed tastings, pop-ups, craft classes and even yoga. You can book an upscale stay on the Driftwood winery grounds at the Wine Country Inn, with complimentary tasting and the option of dinner from a private chef.

Lake Buchanan has long been a destination for recreation: water sports, fishing, hunting, nature exploration and — back when the area was a "wet" oasis surrounded by "dry" counties — honky-tonking. There are scores of vacation and lake cottages; nearby attractions include Longhorn Caverns and the Vanishing Texas Cruises, whose boats ferry nature and history buffs to hidden areas of the lake and the Colorado River and, on one cruise, to Fall Creek.

HAAK VINEYARDS
AND WINERY

6310 Avenue T, Santa Fe. haakwine.com. Contact: 409-925-1401. Tasting room open 11a-5p Mon-Wed, 11a-6p Thu-Sat, noon-5:30p Sun. Tours Fri-Sun, fee includes tasting; call to confirm availability.

Overview

Halfway between Houston and Galveston, in Santa Fe, Texas, Haak Vineyards and Winery sits on 12 acres amid residential streets. The imposing mission-style building that houses the tasting room fronts a road leading to three acres of vineyards, threaded with pathways. Also here is an event space with a commercial-grade kitchen, employing an on-staff chef, that stays fully booked for weddings much of the year. You just don't see a winery of this scale along Texas' Gulf Coast, but here it is.

Andrew Chalk

Raymond Haak in Haak Vineyards and Winery's old-wines cellar.

Haak's mission-style tasting room is the face of the winery, which occupies an unlikely plot halfway between Houston and Galveston.

Philosophy

The Gulf Coast is not a region conducive to the growing of good wine grapes. The Eurasian *vinifera* grapes used to make the wines most of us are familiar with do not flourish here. And then there is Pierce's disease, the scourge most feared by grape-growers everywhere in Texas but the High Plains, where cold weather inhibits its development. Caused by bacteria that cut off a vine's water supply, it will kill a vine within five years. In Texas it is spread by an insect called the glassy-winged sharpshooter, and it is endemic to the Gulf Coast. Very few grapes are resistant to it.

Why, then, given the difficult conditions, would Raymond and Gladys Haak establish their winery in Santa Fe? "Because we were here," he says. Haak (pronounced like *hack*) grew from two grapevines Gladys Haak gave her husband, an engineer in the Houston oil industry, as a wedding-anniversary gift in 1969. It turned out that grapes were their passion, and they began planting more and making wine from them. In 2000, they went commercial as Haak Vineyards and Winery.

Haak's approach is to work with the vines that work where he is. So he began growing blanc du bois, the hybrid grape developed by the University of Florida specifically to be resistant to Pierce's disease. Blanc du bois flourishes in the Gulf Coast's humid climate, but historically it had not been favored by serious winemakers because it produced a white wine without arresting character. Haak began tinkering with his blanc du bois grapes, and he came up with something totally new, a fortified dessert wine. Then he did the same for the hybrid American native grape that flourishes on the Gulf Coast, lenoir (aka jacquez or black Spanish).

These days, Haak also ships in grapes grown in other parts of Texas, mainly the High Plains, and makes the wine here on the Gulf. He is currently sourcing malbec and tempranillo from grower Vijay Reddy in Brownfield in the Texas High Plains AVA. But it is with blanc du bois that he has made his name.

Significant accomplishments

It may be his engineer's background that explains Haak's tinkering approach to blanc du bois. His tinkering got him global acclaim and pretty much enshrined him as one of the significant pioneers of the Texas wine industry. The reason: He invented a whole new category of Texas wine — dessert blanc du bois, made in the style of the famous Portuguese fortified wine madeira.

Before Haak introduced his Texas Madeira, blanc du bois in Texas was either vinified sweet by wineries that sold directly from the cellar door or made into a dry, high-acid wine. The latter style was in direct competition with sauvignon blanc, which was available from producers all over the world, had a lot more name recognition and was sold at prices Texas wineries couldn't compete with.

Haak escaped this price prison by creating a more refined wine from blanc du bois — his Texas Madeira, a blanc du bois submitted to *est-*

The label of the iconoclastic Haak Texas Madeira.

ufagem, a months-long heating process, in his homemade *estufa*, or cooker. The result is an oxidative sweet wine with 17 percent alcohol and a character similar to that of madeira. The esteemed British wine critic Jancis Robinson, editor of *The Oxford Companion to Wine*, reviewed it and scored it "superior." Thus Haak, the boutique winery that started with two grapevines in Santa Fe, Texas, became one of the first Texas wineries to be mentioned in print on two continents.

Best wines

Beyond his blanc du bois Texas Madeira, Haak also took the primary red grape of the Gulf, lenoir — also known as black Spanish and the European name jacquez, which Haak prefers — and made a madeira out of it. Along the way, Haak also subjected the two favored grapes of the Gulf to the same treatment as Portugal's famous port wine. The result was a white port and a red. You will not go wrong with any of these dessert wines, red or white, port or madeira.

Locked up: The old-wines cellar at Haak Vineyards and Winery.

Not content with two dessert categories to his name, however, Haak turned his attention to blanc du bois as a table wine. In 2008, he produced a Blanc du Bois Reserve in which the wine had been aged sur lie — on the lees, the yeast deposits that sink to the bottom — in neutral oak barrels.

The result is a wine with more body and a creaminess that elevates the quality of the flavors above that of conventional blanc du bois. It is one of the best table-wine examples of the grape in the state.

Visitor tips

Haak's stately brick winery building and expansive grounds host frequent events, from concerts and dinners to artisans' markets, food-truck festivals and star-gazing nights — telescopes and astronomers provided along with wine. The Friday-Sunday tours are in demand (reservations required), and you can even request tours with Spanish- or German-speaking guides. Haak has four different wine clubs, all with special perks including access to a members' patio and to member-only events.

HILMY CELLARS

12346 E. U.S. 290, Fredericksburg. hilmywine.com. Contact: 830-644-2482, info@hilmywine.com. Tasting room open 11a-6p Mon-Sat, noon-6p Sun.

Andrew Chalk

Estate vineyard at Hilmy Vineyards winery on US. 290 near Fredericksburg.

Overview

Two-fifths of the way to Johnson City from Fredericksburg on U.S. 290 sits Hilmy Cellars. The tasting room is just a modest Hill Country house flanked by 11 acres of estate vineyard, growing carignan, sangiovese, petit verdot, tannat and tempranillo.

Dodge the napping Great Pyrenees as you enter and head over to the bustling tasting counter where staff explain the range of Hilmy wines on offer. Wines bottled under the Hilmy Cellars label are 100 percent Texas grapes. The second label, Erik Hilmy a.k.a., is used for out-of-state fruit that founder Erik Hilmy decides to work with.

Though he didn't plant his first grapes until 2009, Erik Hilmy has quickly and distinctively established himself as a presence in Texas wine. When talking with him, I feel as though I am talking with the Princeton University philosophy department. He is the most cerebral of Texas winemakers.

That approach extends to his florid wine-naming penchant, with bottles like Persephone, named, as you doubtless knew, after the Greek goddess of spring, queen of the underworld. It is a white Rhône blend of viognier and marsanne and elegant to a fault, best with food like turkey or veal. DO.ZWA.ZO is a phonetic riff on the French phrase meaning "two birds," *deux oiseaux*. Not only is the label uncommunicative in terms of what grapes went into the bottle, if you ask Erik for the formula, you'll find that the information expires with the next vintage. It is just whatever two white French grapes in each particular vintage that strike Erik as being interesting to blend. Go figure. You didn't learn this in marketing class.

Philosophy

Erik Hilmy pursues the "joy of winemaking" with a complete disinterest in prospective commercial acceptance of a wine. This focused pursuit has generated him a devoted set of followers. The group swells each year but still feels like one of those private clubs where you have to join a waiting list and learn a secret handshake.

Significant accomplishments

As he's not one to play the show circuit, Hilmy's triumphs are in the bottle. Should he ever develop an interest in marketing his wines, I would expect them to win gold medals at the tougher national shows such as the San Francisco International Wine Competition and the Finger Lakes International Wine Competition.

In a show of Texas wines to the New York trade in October 2017, Hilmy's wines drew widespread praise.

Best wines

Among whites, the aforementioned Persephone, the Hilmy Cellars Oaked Viognier and Hilmy Cellars Albariño are all the kind of wines you would be proud to serve to the wine buyer at a top restaurant. Among reds, the tempranillo and mourvèdre are wonderful complements to lamb and game.

Visitor tips

Hilmy Cellars is surrounded by a working farm, populated with livestock of both the bovine and ovine variety as well as guinea fowl, peafowl and chickens, not to mention dogs and cats. Don't expect to bring your own pooch, as it might not get along with the resident fauna. (Those with service dogs may call ahead.)

Hilmy's tasting room and patio are far more intimate than grand, so at peak visiting times reservations are advisable; they're required for groups of six or more.

Among the dinners and wine-release parties, keep an eye on the website for Hilmy's late-night Star-Gazing Parties, with guest astronomers, games, a bonfire and s'mores.

Hilmy followers who want to be sure of receiving all the new releases will make sure to maintain their membership in the Hilmy wine club, called the FLOCK (a photo of the resident guinea fowl illustrates the wine-club portion of the winery's website).

INWOOD ESTATES VINEYARDS

Dallas: 1350 Manufacturing St., Suite 209. inwoodwines.com. Contact: 214-902-9452, getinfo@inwoodwines.com. Tasting room open 4-6p Fri (call to confirm), noon-5p Sat. **Fredericksburg:** 10303 U.S. 290, Fredericksburg. inwoodwines.com. Contact: 830-997-2304, InwoodFBG@gmail.com. Tasting room open 11a-5p Sun-Thu, 11a-6p Fri.-Sat. Tasting fee.

Andrew Chalk

Inwood founder Dan Gatlin, foreground, holding a trade tasting at Smith and Wollensky in New York in 2017.

Overview

Driving west from Fredericksburg, at a busy kink in U.S. 290, one winery stands out whose presence looms large in the folklore of Texas wine. Inwood Estates Vineyards prices its Texas wine at up to $225 a bottle and sells out every year. The winery no longer seeks retail accounts, as the mailing list snaps up all the production, with the exception of a few restaurants selected because they loyally signed up for the wines back when sales weren't quite so flush.

The man behind Inwood Estates is Dan Gatlin, who comes by his interest in wine naturally, having grown up in the retail beverage industry. His family owned the Hasty chain of beverage stores in Dallas, and Gatlin worked in the family business until it sold.

Gatlin began his winemaking career back in 1981, when there were only a few dozen wineries in Texas, with an experimental *vinifera* vineyard he planted in Denton County to see what grapes would grow in Texas.

Inwood Estates came into being in 1997, when Gatlin and his wife purchased an old house on a big lot on Inwood Road in Dallas, moved in and planted an "urban vineyard" on the property. Gatlin still maintains a tasting room with limited hours in Dallas, and his estate vineyards are in the High Plains and near Fredericksburg in central Texas, where he lives, but his main presence for the public is on 290.

Along the way to the national acclaim he now commands, he helped establish, in collaboration with grower Neal Newsom, that tempranillo was a great choice of grape to plant in the Texas High Plains. He also proved that chardonnay can do well in Texas, despite its naysayers, and that cabernet sauvignon should not be written off here either.

Philosophy

Dan Gatlin is committed to 100 percent Texas grapes. When he has made wine from grapes from elsewhere, he has not bottled it as Inwood Estates Vineyard wine.

When he began his career as a Texas winemaker, he says, he initially thought that the crucial element of making great wine was great technique. Having been heavily involved in his family's beverage business, he had many ties to the California wine industry, so he implemented as much advice as possible from California winemaking.

But his experimental vineyard in Denton County was a miserable failure. He determined the problem was the terroir — the soil and climate — and began looking to drier climates. Eventually he partnered with grower Newsom in Yoakum County in the Texas High Plains, where the altitude created near-perfect conditions.

Lately, though, his theory of what makes great wine has shifted again. Like University of California Davis professor Mike Matthews, he has become an exponent of the view that great winemaking technique lies in "leveling" the viticultural landscape, making terroir less relevant. This means a breeding program focuses on producing supervines, combined with insanely low yields. It's a controversial theory, but he makes the position credible with chardonnays appellated Dallas County and City of Dallas that have many of the qualities of a Chablis, despite having been grown in the hot climate of north Texas.

Significant accomplishments

It is an article of faith these days that the tempranillo grape is the hitherto most successful grape from the High Plains, but few people realize how instrumental the Gatlin-Newsom collaboration was in establishing that.

Gatlin had long before decided that *vinifera* grapes were the

How to convince the skeptics of the quality of your wine: Dan Gatlin routinely compares his $225 small-production wines, including Magnus, at left, and Colos, second from left, head-to-head with old-world equivalents.

way to go when he took over winemaking at the Vineyard at Florence, next to his estate vineyards, in 2009. There, however, he was charged with an already planted vineyard that included some blanc du bois, a hybrid of *vinifera* and native American grapes developed to resist Pierce's disease but known for producing boring, foxy sauvignon blanc wannabes.

Gatlin crafted a new expression of the grape, giving it more mouthfeel and flavors of peach and tropical fruit, resulting in a somewhat southern Rhône character.

From the vineyard he established behind his old house on In-

Inwood Estates Winery makes exceptional chardonnay from grapes grown in Dallas County and a palomino blend that adds Hunt County grapes. Both represent a triumph of expert winemaking over established wisdom regarding terroir.

wood Road in Dallas, he made a Chablis-style chardonnay (likewise with a vineyard on Bear Creek Road in Dallas County that eventually fell to developers).

In later years, Gatlin reduced yields to unheard-of levels (0.3 tons/acre in one case) to make tempranillo and cabernet sauvignon wines of intense power that sold out at more than $200 retail.

Best wines

To sample the Inwood style, you would do well to start with the latest vintage of the "Cornelius" Tempranillo ($50). Inwood also makes exceptional chardonnay.

To taste the best, the Colos (100 percent tempranillo) and Magnus (a tempranillo-cabernet blend), each $225, are the ultimate expression of the Inwood Estates mission.

Visitor tips

The Fredericksburg tasting room offers a variety of settings, including the Bistro & Wine Bar, where cheese boards and barbecue lunches are available; an outdoor deck; and a pet-friendly area called the Grove. A reserve tasting room is open on Saturdays, when you can also book two different special tastings with Gatlin in attendance. For the Super Flight, he puts some of his limited-availability wines up against European wines.

The urban tasting room in Dallas' Design District behind the Anatole Hotel is usually open Friday evening and Saturday afternoon, but best call ahead to be sure.

Membership in one of the four limited-membership levels of the Inwood Club Wine Guild assures you allocations of new releases and gets you various perks throughout the year, including tickets to the festive Winemaker's Christmas Party.

KIEPERSOL VINEYARDS AND WINERY

3933 FM 344 E., Tyler. kiepersol.com. Contact: 903-894-8995, winery@kiepersol.com. Tasting room open 11a-7p Tue-Sat. Guided public tours of winery and distillery at 2 and 4p Sat; guided winery tours 1p Tue-Fri (fee).

Kiepersol Enterprises

Marnelle Durrett, Kiepersol proprietor and founding winemaker.

Overview

By all rights, Kiepersol Vineyards and Winery should not exist. Kiepersol is the remarkable grower of 16 *Vitis vinifera* grape varieties near Tyler in East Texas, an area singularly famous for not being suitable for *Vitis vinifera* wine grapes. Indeed, Kiepersol has more than 60 acres of these grapes and uses this estate vineyard to source all the wines it makes.

Credit for this achievement goes to founder Pierre de Wet, a transplanted South African farmer who emigrated to the United States and found Kiepersol's

Kiepersol Enterprises

The late Pierre de Wet, founder of Kiepersol Estates.

unique location at the top of a salt dome. It was de Wet's belief that the salt dome produces changes in the magnetic field, causing storms to split around the dome as they move through the area and thus protecting the vineyards from storm damage. He began planting vines there at the end of the 1990s.

After his passing in 2016, the running of the winery — and quite a little empire of peripheral activities, including a B&B, a restaurant, a distillery, an upscale RV park and a conference and event center with a recording studio — fell to his daughters, Marnelle Durrett and Velmay Powers, who have maintained the high standards.

Philosophy

Kiepersol reflects Pierre de Wet's philosophy of agriculture; every Kiepersol wine is 100 percent Texas grapes and 100 percent estate-grown. All its grapes are *Vitis vinifera*, the species of grapes that makes the best wines in the world; while the Latin terminology may be obscure, the grapes are the most familiar names in the wine store: sauvignon blanc, pinot grigio, viognier, muscat of Alexandria and semillon account for the whites; cabernet franc, cabernet sauvignon, malbec, merlot, mourvèdre, tempranillo, sangiovese and syrah the reds.

"My father's philosophies of living debt-free and making people happy by sharing passions of food, wine, spirits and place, while holding on to our core values of serving each other and our guests with love, have not changed," said Durrett, the founding winemaker. "His beliefs set the foundation for what we continue to do every day."

Significant achievements

That Kiepersol has been a somewhat hidden gem partly reflects de Wet's view that his wines would become known through word of mouth. One modest change with the transition to the new generation is that the winery is entering more wine competitions. It is little surprise that the winery is also winning medals. It was named 2017 Top Texas Winery by the Houston Livestock Show and Rodeo International Wine Competition.

Among its many other awards, in recent years the winery has brought home double golds (unanimous jury selection) for its 2009 merlot, its 2010 Barrel No. 33 red blend and its 2011 Mengsel Bordeaux-style blend.

And Kiepersol's small-batch whiskey, rum and vodka have also garnered a slew of gold and silver medals at national contests, including the San Francisco World Spirits Competition.

The biggest environmental risk to *Vitis vinifera* grapes in East Texas is Pierce's disease, which is spread by an insect called the glassy-winged sharpshooter. Pierre de Wet had an innovative solution to the threat: zinc sprayed onto the vines to protect them. The solution drew interest from the Texas Department of Agriculture, as Kiepersol appeared to be the only winery able to successfully grow *vinifera* in the area.

Best wines

My top choices among Kiepersol's wines are the syrah, tempranillo, sauvignon blanc and Steen (chenin blanc).

Visitor tips

The wine is only the beginning at the Kiepersol compound — you could probably spend a week's vacation at Kiepersol without running out of things to do. Reserve a room at the B&B (or one of three other opulently furnished accommodations on the grounds) and a dinner seating at the Restaurant at Kiepersol, which offers classic American steakhouse-style fine dining. Or sip a dram at the Distillery at Kiepersol, which crafts small-batch vodka, whiskey and rum.

In 2014, the operation added Salt Kitchen, a stadium-seating demonstration kitchen where it offers tastings, demonstrations and cooking and crafts classes. Kiepersol maintains a busy schedule of vinters' dinners, parties, holiday celebrations and wine education classes, along with sponsoring regular running events.

In spring, folks drive through the verdant, rolling countryside around Tyler to view azaleas and dogwoods in bloom, but it's roses that put the city on the map. At 14 acres, the Tyler Municipal Rose Garden is billed as the largest rose garden in the country. And on one weekend in October, the entire city goes rose-wild during the venerable Texas Rose Festival, a Southern-style extravaganza complete with elaborate rose displays, a fair, plant sale, art shows,

Kiepersol Restaurant and B&B entrance.

teas, ladies' and men's luncheons, *two* coronation ceremonies for the Rose Queen and a parade with Mardi-Gras-worthy ball gowns and costumes.

LEWIS WINES

3209 U.S. 290, Johnson City. lewiswines.com. Contact: 512-987-0660, kyle@lewiswines.com. Tasting room open 10:30a-5p daily; reservations suggested; tasting fee refunded with two-bottle purchase. Tours 10a Sat.

Copyright © Michael Lecuona

Doug Lewis with harvested grapes at Lewis Wines.

Overview

As you accelerate out of Johnson City, traveling west on U.S. 290 toward Fredericksburg, watch for the big propane tanks on the south side of the road. The entrance soon after on the left, marked by oak barrels and some large boulders, is Lewis Wines. Follow the driveway around a house and up a rise where, near a limestone hill, sits the concrete-walled winery with an outdoor pavilion of reclaimed wood. Doug Lewis, after whom the winery is named, and co-owner Duncan McNabb run the show.

It didn't take more than a few years for these two to make a name for themselves as the latest wunderkinds in the Texas wine world. Lewis is a Texas winery with a clear mission: to produce the best wine it can from Texas grapes. Already, Lewis has established itself as a name to watch.

Lewis Wines started in 2009 as a magpie in the attic at nearby Pedernales Cellars, where Doug Lewis worked his way up from harvest intern to cellar rat, tour guide and vineyard worker. In 2012, operations moved to the current location where they opened a modern winemaking facility and later a tasting room. Bottling rose from 400 cases in 2010 to 5,000 in 2017.

They currently buy grapes from some well-known Texas vineyards, including Lost Draw Vineyards, Newsom Vineyards and Phillips Vineyard, all in the High Plains AVA; and Parr Vineyards, Round Mountain Vineyard and Tallent Vineyards, in the Hill Country AVA. The 100-year devastating frost in the High Plains in 2013 forced some last-minute adjustments in procurement practices, including trips to East Texas, where they acquired some blanc du bois grapes at Enoch's Stomp Vineyard & Winery. Lewis used the grapes to make a Portuguese-style vinho-verde-inspired white, and all of a sudden Lewis' summery Swim Spot was everywhere.

Lewis' grape preferences lean toward Spanish and Portuguese varieties. Among reds, that includes tempranillo, touriga nacional, tinto cão, mourvèdre, syrah, cabernet franc and graciano. Whites include chenin blanc, albariño and blanc du bois. If you're lucky, you might come across a bottle of arinto, now in small production. Other varieties in the ground as part of Lewis' ambitious planting program at its estate vineyard are tannat and alicanté bouschet.

There is clearly an emphasis on Iberian grape varieties, with the Portuguese tilt helping set Lewis Wines apart.

Philosophy

"Every successful wine industry relies on the collaboration between wineries and growers," Lewis says.

He and McNabb don't wait for the growers they buy from to pick the grapes; they take that job into their own hands to allow them more control. When they decide the time is right, their employees, along with friends and relatives, all wearing headlamps, head out after midnight to harvest the grapes at whatever vineyard is ready. The goal is to finish processing the fruit back at the winery by sunrise.

This proactive practice ensures quality while minimizing the risk for the grower, who might not be able to nail down a picking crew at the exact time the grapes are at their best.

"I think any winery winemaker who takes more control over the harvest is more likely to make good wine," Lewis said.

Significant accomplishments

In 2018, *Wine Enthusiast* named Lewis Winery as one of three Texas Hill Country operations to visit, along with Duchman Family Winery and Pedernales Cellars. "A new generation of Texas winemakers has been making its mark at Lewis Wines," the national wine magazine raved.

In 2017, the Wine & Food Foundation of Texas named Lewis Wines' 2012 Cabernet Sauvignon-Tempranillo Newsom Vineyards as the "Texas Wine of the Year."

From 2014 through 2017, Lewis received gold medals at the TEXSOM International Wine Awards for mourvèdre, viognier and tempranillo wines and a "best of show" for its 2011 Round Mountain Vineyard Reserve made from a single Portuguese variety, touriga nacional.

If a Texas restaurant has more than one or two token Texas-made wines on its list, chances are Lewis will be represented; the winery's Swim Spot has been a major commercial success.

Lewis Wines' adventurous pursuit of excellence in so many varieties epitomizes the ambition of the latest generation of young winemakers around the state.

Best wines

I have tasted wines from Lewis over several vintages, and they show a consistent trend toward improvement each year they are made. Lewis and McNabb have quickly become among the most proficient winemakers in the state. Their dry rosé made from hand-picked, whole-cluster-pressed mourvèdre and grenache is a top seller, and I especially recommend that buyers look for their tempranillo offerings, their mourvèdre and their viognier.

Visitor tips

The winery's tasting roster changes constantly, and the pavilion never seems too crowded. Unlike tasting rooms where servers are hired only to work behind the counter, those at Lewis Wines also work in the vineyard and winery, which means these cross-trained staffers know what they are talking about from hands-on experience. Guests can bring their own food or order platters of cheese from such craft producers as Lipan's Eagle Mountain Farmhouse Cheese, with bread from Fredericksburg's Bakery JoJu.

There are events for wine club members, every-other-Friday reserve tastings (except during harvest) and occasional live music. The winery throws an old-fashioned crawfish boil (Lewis' father hails from Louisiana) with a zydeco band every spring to celebrate the release of its new rosés.

LLANO ESTACADO WINERY

llanowine.com. Contact: 800-634-3854, info@llanowine.com. Tasting room open noon-6p Tue-Fri, 1-5p Sat-Sun. Tours every half-hour; last tour at 4p.

Llano Estacado Winery

A new tasting room and an expansive event center are part of the changes at Llano Estacado Winery, which occupies a unique place in Texas wine history and has evolved along with the state's wine industry.

Overview

Llano Estacado Winery is the second-largest winery in Texas (after Mesa Vineyards, which produces Ste. Genevieve), selling 165,000 cases per year at press time. It is also one of the oldest, having been founded on the plains near Lubbock in 1976 by Texas Tech chemistry professors Clinton "Doc" McPherson and Robert

"Bob" Reed to market the results of their then-novel experiments in cultivating *vinifera* vines. It is recognized by the state as the first bonded Texas winery to have opened since Prohibition.

The winery's most recent expansion added a Napa-quality tasting room and visitor center and retooled the original winery building as an impressive event center, particularly popular hereabouts for weddings. When you visit the new tasting room, step into the adjacent original winery and note that the walls are made of six-inch cinderblock. That wasn't for insulation or protection from tornadoes, it was because McPherson thought that prohibitionists in the local population might shoot up his winery.

With Doc's son Kim McPherson as winemaker, Llano helped put Texas on the American wine map when its 1984 chardonnay won a double gold at the San Francisco Fair's International Wine Competition. Over time, however, ownership transfers, inheritances and other factors resulted in the privately held operation being split into many different parcels. The good news is that developments in recent years have shown that this relative heavyweight is nevertheless nimble enough to pivot adroitly to face the new realities of the wine business in Texas.

The story of the modern Llano Estacado starts in 1993, when the owners began the process of building new leadership. From California they brought in the highly credentialed Greg Bruni to supervise the winemaking. Soon Mark Hyman, having years of sales experience with several major wine and spirits conglomerates, joined up to drive the marketing. Small at the time, Llano was nonetheless well-funded. To both men, this looked like an opportunity they could take by the scruff of the neck and build to a much larger case turnover and quality reputation. It turned out they arrived at just the right time. They are still at the helm today.

Philosophy

Llano's changes hold lessons for other Texas wineries, particularly those growing to the point of mass-marketing their wines. Bruni and Hyman set out to make and sell the best wine they could from Texas grapes. To increase volume, they supplemented Texas grapes with out-of-state fruit for aggressively priced supermarket brands, but they also began to endorse the idea of making wine from the types of grapes that grow best in Texas. They saw Llano's best wines winning medals at top out-of-state wine competitions and acclaim from national publications.

Llano Estacado Winery

Technique is a major focus for Llano Estacado executive winemaker Greg Bruni, left, and winemaker Jason Centanni, seen here tasting wine in barrel. Centanni employs some expensive laboratory tools, including an OenoFoss analyzer to monitor some 40 simultaneous fermentations.

Nowadays, Llano cultivates relationships with Texas growers and makes more than 50 wines, representing more than 23 grape varieties. Diversification of grape sourcing is used as a defense against frost years. Only its cheapest supermarket sweet wines are from out-of-state fruit. This is a significant shift for a large ship.

Llano's central relationship nowadays is the one with growers. Two High Plains growers, Reddy Vineyards and Newsom Vineyard, figure prominently in the winery's sourcing. Newsom provides the sangiovese for the product-line-leading Viviano, a Tuscan blend of the best cabernet sauvignon from a given vintage with 25 to 30 percent sangiovese, as well as the merlot for the Cellar Reserve Merlot. Reddy Vineyards supplies all the grapes for Due Compaesani (sangiovese-montepulciano) and the Signature Rosé. Both provide grapes for Llano's Pinot Grigio, THP Tempranillo and THP Stampede, a nontraditional red blend.

As if to prove that vines thrive under adversity, the Dell Valley Vineyard, at an elevation of 4,000 feet in the Chihuahuan Desert east of El Paso, grows chardonnay, chenin blanc, gewürztraminer, grenache, muscat, riesling and syrah, all of which go into premium wines at Llano.

Technique is also a major focus for Bruni and winemaker Jason Centanni, whose background is in biochemistry. They have installed expensive micro-oxygenation equipment at the winery. Micro-ox, as it is called, is controversial among winemakers: It reduces tannin by adding oxygen in carefully controlled amounts to red wine during fermentation, making the mouthfeel softer and the aroma and bouquet more complex, so that the wine seems more mature and readier to drink upon release.

Significant accomplishments

Llano can lay claim to a number of major accomplishments in the Texas wine industry in the last quarter-century: Setting the standard for fine wine, innovation in winemaking, creating first-class visitor facilities in the High Plains and projecting Texas wines into ordinary Texas homes through supermarket and other retail sales as well as high-end restaurants have all been among them.

Best wines

In 2018 *Wine Enthusiast* magazine gave three of Llano's rosés ratings in the high 80s: 89 for the Monte Stella and Signature (rated a best buy at $10) and 87 for the Mont Sec.

Tastings of Llano's best wines underscore the quality focus. The flagship Viviano and all the wines with a vineyard designation on the front label are especially recommended. This winery is committed to quality and one of the wineries in the lead in Texas' entry onto the national wine stage.

Visitor tips

Though tastings are free, you will find plenty to purchase in the expansive wood-floored tasting room studded with bottle racks and gift displays. A wrap-around patio overlooks the surrounding cotton fields. Tours are free too, running on the half-hour six days a week.

Llano is closed on Mondays, and occasionally on other days for private or wine-club events, so check the calendar on the website before your visit. In 2015 Llano built a big dedicated event center overlooking the estate vineyard, and weddings and other private events are a major part of its business.

Llano Estacado offers three wine club options — sweet, mixed and red — with perks that include complimentary tastings for the member and three guests each quarter, wine discounts, parties and custom wine-label designs.

McPHERSON CELLARS

1615 Texas Ave., Lubbock. mcphersoncellars.com. Contact: 806-687-9463, info@mcphersoncellars.com. Tastings and tours: 11a-6p Mon-Sat (reservations required for six or more).

Angela Guthrie

Kim McPherson in the vineyard.

Overview

There may be no one alive more pivotal to Texas winemaking than Kim McPherson.

An enology student at America's best winemaking school, the University of California Davis, McPherson emerged from the shadow of his famous father, Clinton "Doc" McPherson (who, with Robert Reed, first grew *vinifera* grapes commercially in Texas).

Kim McPherson was the winemaker when his father's Llano Estacado Winery won a double gold in San Francisco for its chardonnay; after that, he spent 16 years as winemaker for Lubbock's CapRock. He has his own wine label and has made wine for literally dozens of Texas wineries on a contract basis. When noted California winemaker Dave Phinney decided to add "TX" wine to his Locations brand, he chose McPherson to make it with him.

McPherson maintains a Lubbock tasting room and a major presence in one of the Hill Country's most popular tasting rooms, 4.0 Cellars. In Lubbock, his home base, he converted a 1930s art-moderne Coca-Cola bottling plant on the edge of downtown Lubbock's nightlife/arts district, the Depot District, into a winery with a striking tasting room and a pleasant patio. With its colorful, playful urban feel, the winery offers a refreshing contrast to the faux-Italianate-villa look so many Texas wineries affect.

In the Hill Country, McPherson is a principal in the 4.0 Cellars collaboration with Brennan Vineyards and Lost Oak Vineyards. On a strategic bend of U.S. 290, the 4.0 tasting room attracts crowds on weekends with its large outdoor area and live entertainment.

Philosophy

McPherson makes great wine, both for his own label and within his clients' requirements. He has been a major promoter of Texas grapes, using them almost exclusively, and was an early Texas proponent of "planting to the land," these days using warm-climate Rhône, Italian and French grape varieties.

He believes in keeping his wines accessible and affordable — resulting in some great bargains — but he's always experimenting with something new — building a solera at his winery to make sherry, just for one example.

Significant accomplishments

McPherson's own label has significant restaurant presence, and the Locations brand's "TX" wine has become a colossal marketing success.

Mentor, collaborator and one of the most respected men within the Texas wine industry, McPherson has helped establish the reputations of numerous Texas wineries — Lost Draw Cellars, Trilogy Cellars and Crossroads Winery among them. It is safe to say the Texas wine industry would not be what it is today without Kim McPherson.

Best wines

From his own label, I think the McPherson Roussanne Reserve sets the standard for Texas roussanne. It is a bargain relative to West Coast offerings but in the same quality league, and it is the wine I take as an unannounced present to winemakers when I visit the Rhône.

Angela Guthrie

A selection of Kim McPherson's wines.

Visitor tips

McPherson's downtown Lubbock tasting room maintains a lively roster of events, including Thursday night live music on the patio from May to September and participation in the downtown arts district's First Friday Art Trail.

Should you be feeling peckish, just around the corner is the delightful La Diosa Cellars, a quirky, exuberantly appointed tapas bistro that may be the most rewarding spot to nosh in Lubbock and happens to be owned by McPherson's wife, Sylvia.

PEDERNALES CELLARS

2916 Upper Albert Road, Stonewall. pedernalescellars.com. Contact: 830-644-2037, tastingroom@pedernalescellars.com. Estate tasting room open 10a-5p Mon-Thu, to 6p Fri-Sat, noon-5p Sun; reservations requested Sat and for groups of more than six. Main Street Tasting Room, 134 E. Main St., Fredericksburg, open 11a-6p daily; reservations requested for groups of more than six. Tasting fee; various levels of tastings available by appointment; tours by appointment.

Pedernales Cellars

Picnickers enjoy the Hill Country view outside Pedernales Cellars' tasting room.

Overview

Pedernales Cellars started as the 17-acre Kuhlken Vineyard, planted in the early 1990s by Larry and Jeanine Kuhlken on the Llano highway north of Fredericksburg. Years of experimentation produced consistent, excellent fruit. In 2006, the next generation took the next step: The Kuhlkens' children, David and Julie, along with spouses Heather Kuhlken and Fredrik Osterberg, respectively, founded Pedernales Cellars as an artisan producer of high-quality Texas wines.

David Kuhlken had attended the nation's top enology and viticulture school, the University of California Davis. Julie and Fredrik had academic and business experience and ran the marketing and sales side of the winery. Julie continues to manage marketing and sales since Fredrik's departure from the winery in 2016.

The winery is set back about two miles from U.S. 290. The tasting room is a Napa-quality operation set atop a rise that affords spectacular views from the front patio. Despite being off U.S. 290 proper, Pedernales is popular with visitors and can be a mass of cars and limos on Saturday afternoons, when you'll need a reservation for a tasting.

The winery's popularity led the Kuhlkens to create a presence in the middle of all the tourist action in nearby Fredericksburg with their Main Street Tasting Room, which is open daily.

Pedernales has acquired an enviable reputation for its wines, which are now in wide distribution throughout the state and among the most common Texas wines to see on restaurant wine lists. When its no-compromise approach to quality pushed prices above $25, instead of cutting costs on its flagship wines, the winery wisely introduced a second label, Armadillo's Leap. These wines, still Texas-sourced, are described as "your go-to Texas wine for everyday sipping," with prices around half that of the Pedernales Cellars wines.

Philosophy

The goal at Pedernales is the best Texas wine they can make, and the creation of the second label has freed their hands to do this. The winery focuses on grapes that have been shown to grow well in Texas, including those from its estate vineyard, and has built up long-term relationships with several growers, including Bingham, Newsom and Reddy from the High Plains; Stout Vineyard, owned by master sommelier Guy Stout just south of Blanco; and Speier Vineyards, a meticulously cultivated Texas Hill Country AVA vineyard.

Significant accomplishments

Pedernales pioneered the idea of a "reserve" tasting experience in Texas: You pay extra for the winery's very best wines, service from a sommelier with a wine certification and separate sit-down setting. The idea is now widely copied. Paying for this is a no-brainer if you have flown or driven in from outside the local area.

The Kuhlkens are also deeply committed to sustainability in all aspects of their wine production; a geothermal system cools the cellar and case storage, refurbished barrels are used and compost from the winery goes back onto the vineyards. On the grounds, removal of invasive species like cedar has been a priority, restoring water flow to seeps and springs.

Best wines

The Pedernales Reserve Viognier is one of the best viogniers from Texas. In a very ripe, lush style with ample oak, the 2012 vintage was the only American wine to score a double gold at the 2013 Lyon International Wine Competition. It won a sommeliers' blind tasting of 19 viogniers — including a top French bottle and two strong California ones, along with 15 other Texas bottles — I put together in 2013. The Pedernales Reserve Tempranillo won a similar tasting of 23 tempranillos. Pedernales' GSM is also a substantial wine.

Visitor tips

Call ahead if you're thinking of attending the reserve tasting on a Saturday — you'll need a reservation to make sure you're on the list. There's a lounge for wine club members and several levels of reserve and private tastings, including the barrel-tasting tours hosted on Saturdays.

Andrew Chalk

Saturdays and Sundays also bring live music, and Pedernales' weekend grape stomps during harvest draw enthusiastic crowds. If the parking lot is packed, you can drop off and pick up your group in a special area at the tasting-room front door, and there's handicapped parking and a ramp.

PERISSOS VINEYARD AND WINERY

7214 Park Road 4 W., Burnet. perissosvineyards.com. Contact: 512-820-2950, Laura@PerissosVineyards.com. Tasting room open noon-5p Thu-Sun. Tasting fee, waived with three-bottle purchase. Tours by appointment.

Perissos Vineyard and Winery

A vertical tasting of Perissos tempranillos dating from 2009 to 2015. The wines, tasted at the winery in January 2018, were all superbly made and showed long aging potential.

Overview

In 1999, Laura and Seth Martin were living in Austin, where they had established a successful custom homebuilding business. They decided to plant some grapes on their land and started making wine in their garage as a hobby. Soon they began to realize that they had fallen in love with wine and winemaking and wanted to do it full-time.

Eventually, the family found 42 acres of decomposed granite soil just south of Inks Lake and became full-time farmers, grape-growers and winemakers. They brought in their first harvest in 2006, built a dramatic stone farmhouse-style building and moved in above the winery, opening for business in 2009 (a couple of expansions have taken place since). It was "a place where we and our children could run free, get dirty, work hard and savor the land," the Martins note on their website. The vineyard has grown to 16 acres today, planted to *vinifera* grapes.

Philosophy

Perissos' philosophy is front and center on the winery's home page: "Locally grown and true to Texas." Ever since the first vintage, Perissos wines have been made from 100 percent Texas-grown grapes. Through years in which other wineries made excuses, Perissos grew or contracted enough fruit to keep that promise. Some three-quarters of their grapes come from their own vineyards (the rest is contracted from other Texas growers). The Martins practice organic and sustainable cultivation methods; originally, all their grapes were hand-harvested, though they have succumbed to some mechanical picking.

The Perissos website further explains the Martins' winemaking philosophy: "Being winemakers as well as farmers for the vast majority of the wines we produce, we have a simple philosophy in the creation and development of the wines. We believe that 99 percent of the work in creating the wines occurs in the vineyard."

Significant accomplishments

Seth Martin is a self-taught viticulturist and enologist. In an environment in which vineyards die from Pierce's disease and other threats, he and Laura have managed to keep their 16 acres of estate vines vibrant and productive. Their medal count reflects this, with six medals from out-of-state wine competitions in 2014, seven in 2015, 10 in 2016, six in 2017 and five in 2018. They've notched four best-of-class wins in the *San Francisco Chronicle* Wine Competition.

Best wines

Among the whites, the roussanne represents a rich, ripe, fruit-forward expression of this northern Rhône grape. The ripeness contributes substance to the mouthfeel, making this wine a fine match to lobster, pork or other white meat.

Aglianico, from the estate vineyard, is the best red. This grape originated in southern Italy, Campania and Basilicata, where it makes full-bodied wines with redoubtable tannins and longevity. It has taken to several warm climates around the world, including Texas, but the grape's success in Texas is little-known outside the state, likely due to the tiny acreage produced. Friends knowledgeable about this grape with whom I've shared Perissos' aglianico have been blown away by the varietal correctness and the overall winemaking quality displayed by the Perissos wine.

Visitor tips

Long rows of vines march right up to the big sandstone building that houses Perissos' winery and tasting room. Things are pretty laid-back here; you can bring a picnic (no outside alcohol) and have it at a picnic table or purchase cheese plates to nibble on. You can bring your dog, if you keep it leashed and outdoors; you can

Seth Martin, who founded Perissos with his wife, Laura, estimates shoot-growing potential in a trellis at the winery.

even bring your kids (the Martins have five of their own), if you keep a close eye on them. It's a family farm, after all.

Private tours and tastings can be arranged by reservation.

RON YATES WINES

6676 U.S. 290 West, Hye. ronyateswines.com. Contact: 512-585-3972, info@ronyateswines.com. Tasting room open 11a-6p daily.

Ron Yates' winery and tasting pavilion sit on 16 acres near Hye.

Overview

It would appear that Hye's Ron Yates Wines, which started life as Yates Wines in 2016, has emerged onto the Texas winemaking scene in record time. In fact, owner Ron Yates has been running Spicewood Vineyards, just 35 miles away in the northern reaches of the Hill Country, for more than a decade, after his family purchased it from the founders.

But Ron Yates Wines is his baby. The property covers almost 16 acres, four of them planted in tempranillo grapes (Yates favors Spanish varieties). Yates has built a handsome stone winery building and tasting pavilion crowned with standing-seam tin roofing on the north side of U.S. 290 just east of Hye. Armed with the latest equipment and lots of room to expand, he can eventually produce 20,000 cases yearly, if he chooses (he's doing 10,000 now). His early results have been spectacular, with a slew of medals already to his credit.

To look at Ron Yates, you might guess him to be the lead singer in a Deep-Purple-style rock band. In fact, before he became a winery honcho, he spent some time in the music biz, as a founding partner in the High Wire Music label in Austin.

Yates grew up in a farming family not far from Fall Creek Vineyards, where his relatives Ed and Susan Auler had established themselves as Texas wine pioneers. He trained in the law but never practiced. He had gotten the wine bug in earnest during his college years, while traveling in Spain, where he spent time in the vineyards of the Ribera del Duero region, and it wouldn't let him go. So, in 2007, he took over the helm when his family bought Spicewood.

At his winery here on 290, Yates prefers to stick to the CEO role, employing a professional winemaker, Todd Crowell, who has been making his mark in the same position at Spicewood since 2012.

Philosophy

Texas fruit — both his own and from established growers — currently accounts for all the white wines, almost all the rosé wines and around half the red wines that Ron Yates currently makes. The remainder are made from grapes sourced from northern California (Sonoma's Dry Creek Valley and Russian River Valley) and

Washington (Horse Heaven Hills). They are clearly labeled as such. Yates explains that he loves pinot noir and winemaker Todd Crowell loves zinfandel, so Yates will continue the arduous process of picking up grapes from California with double-teamed drivers in a refrigerator truck and bringing them back to Hye.

As with its sister winery, Spicewood, Ron Yates is a winery that celebrates family. Each of its wines is prominently marked with one of several stylized brands that represent different family members.

Andrew Chalk

Ron Yates at his winery.

Significant accomplishments

Winemaker Crowell is among a small but growing number of Texas winemakers experimenting with the tricky pétillant-naturel style of sparkling wine.

In the winery's short life, medals from the Los Angeles International Wine Competition as well as a significant number of medals from Texas competitions augur well for the future. The experience Yates gained at Spicewood Vineyards has resulted in consistently clean and varietally correct wines.

Best wines

Among the whites, I recommend the viognier, sauvignon blanc and albariño; among the reds, garnacha, mourvèdre and tempranillo, plus the cinsault rosé.

Visitor tips

Keep an eye on the winery's web and Facebook pages for new developments; Yates and Crowell are just getting started. In the works are bigger hospitality spaces, including a club room for private tastings; an underground cellar; and maybe even a swimming pool with rentable cabanas on the grounds.

Saturdays usually bring music by acoustic troubadours and Texas barbecue from a local pitmaster. You can schlep a sandwich out from the rustic-hip Hye Market in town.

Ron Yates charges no membership fees for its three tiers of wine club membership, which come with varying levels of perks and promotions.

WEDDING OAK WINERY

weddingoakwinery.com. **San Saba:** 316 E. Wallace St. Contact: 325-372-4050, info@weddingoakwinery.com. Tasting room open 11a-6p Mon-Thu, 10a-6p Fri-Sat, 11a-5p Sun. **Wedding Oak Winery Burnet** (opening spring 2019): 229 S. Pierce St., Burnet.

Andrew Chalk

Mike McHenry of Wedding Oak Winery has quietly become an important figure on the Texas wine scene.

Overview

Cradled by the San Saba River and surrounded by sandy pecan bottoms on the northern fringe of the Hill Country, San Saba is one of the most appealing small towns in Texas. With a picturesque millpond and a clutch of limestone and sandstone buildings emblematic of turn-of-the-century Texas, its downtown seems steeped in time. But things are stirring in San Saba, and Wedding Oak Winery is right in the heart of it all.

That is by design, according to owner Mike McHenry. He is as enthusiastic about invigorating downtown San Saba as he is in running a winery. To that end, in 2010 he engaged a group of friends to invest in what he expected to call San Saba Wine Cellars. A copyright issue necessitated a name change, and McHenry chose Wedding Oak Winery, in homage to a centuries-old oak tree north of town known historically as a site for wedding ceremonies.

Purchasing three buildings just yards from the junction of U.S. 190 and Texas 16, the main routes through town, McHenry installed state-of-the-art fermenters and a barrel-aging room and built a welcoming stone-walled tasting room that offers a cool haven from the outside sun.

McHenry has been around the Texas wine industry a lot longer than Wedding Oak's short history would suggest. He bought 115 acres in the area in 1998 and started thinking about planting grapes. He approached neighbor Jim Johnson, owner of the nearby Alamosa Wine Cellars and a respected name in Texas winemaking, for advice. Johnson was kind to his friend, explaining from his own experience in the area that McHenry would have to be mad to plant wine grapes. McHenry persisted, however, and Johnson became his viticulture mentor. Johnson was one of Texas' early advocates of warm-climate grape varietals, and he advised McHenry to plant Mediterranean grapes. When McHenry did, Johnson began buying them for his own winery.

Wedding Oak's tasting room opened in June 2012. McHenry staked out his station as CEO of the winery, putting the winemaking in the capable hands of Penny Adams. A graduate of Texas A&M and Fresno State, Adams casts a long shadow in the Texas wine industry. She was one of the first female winemakers in Texas, operating Cypress Valley Vineyard & Winery near Round Mountain from 1981 to 1986, and she served as one of four Texas viticultural advisors before those state jobs were eliminated in 2011.

She brings a deep knowledge of Texas vineyards and grape-growers, and the winery currently sources from several vineyards, including McHenry's Cherokee Creek and High Valley vineyards and Mirasol Vineyard in Lampasas County.

Adams' first release was a quintet of wines made from viognier, muscat canelli, vermentino, trebbiano, sangiovese and tempranillo; subsequent releases have added carignan, grenache, syrah, mourvèdre, cinsault, dolcetto, montepulciano, albariño, graciano and tannat.

Along the way, Wedding Oak has assembled an impressive trophy cabinet, taking awards from the Houston Livestock Show and Rodeo International, Lone Star International and TEXSOM competitions in Texas and from the prestigious San Francisco International, *San Francisco Chronicle* and Finger Lakes competitions on a wider stage.

Look for the latest Wedding Oak iteration, a tasting room and small production facility with a rooftop deck and an opening date of spring 2019, in the historic 1888 Badger Building on the square in Burnet. In the Fredericksburg wine corridor, though McHenry is closing his Wildseed Farms tasting room, he plans to maintain a presence at a new site to be determined; check Wedding Oak's website, weddingoakwinery.com, for updates.

Philosophy

"We believe in using 100 percent Texas-grown grapes to create the best wines possible that reflect our Texas terroir," says McHenry. He and winemaker Adams prefer to explore different varietals among warm-climate grapes rather than just sticking with the tried and true: "We're still looking at different varietals," he says.

"We don't think there's a national wine of Texas yet."

McHenry clearly enjoys the hunt, which lately has looked toward the south of Italy. The winery's first negroamaro release — "inky, dark," notes McHenry with pleasure — is imminent.

Having wasted no time in establishing the winery's reputation, McHenry and Adams are narrowing their focus and steering Wedding Oak toward smaller-lot premium wines for exclusive release to wine club members, while still maintaining the quality of their signature wines. McHenry sells direct to consumer and is "not particularly interested in restaurant wine lists," he says, preferring a personal "two-way, longer-term relationship" with customers.

"We don't have any desire to be up in the $75 or $80 or $90 range," McHenry explains; his goal is to make a $30 or $40 wine of such merit that tasters will say, "This wine is surprisingly affordable."

"We're investing on the wine quality side," McHenry says, and to that end the winery recently brought Cornell master's grad Seth Urbanek on board as assistant winemaker to Adams.

Significant accomplishments

The quality of Wedding Oak's wines is drawing plenty of attention; for the winery's young age, it has racked up an impressive number of top awards in important competitions.

McHenry and Adams have been active in "incubating" new wineries across Texas, starting at home with Old Man Scary Cellars, which occupies a tasting room owned by McHenry in the same historic block as Wedding Oak's in San Saba. Building on that success, Wedding Oak is now working with some half-dozen start-up and established wineries around the state, providing winemaking, viticulture and business services in varying combinations.

McHenry, in short, has quietly become an important figure on the Texas wine scene, a stature solidified in 2018 when he agreed to take over as president of the Texas Wine and Grape Growers Association.

Best wines

To get a crack at Wedding Oak's very best bottles, you might think about joining one of its wine clubs. The winery's portfolio of white wines is particularly strong across the board (and includes some well-made

Andrew Chalk

Wedding Oak's Bridal Blush, a semi-sweet muscat blend from High Plains fruit, is one of its signature wines.

medium-sweet and sweet choices to cover all the bases). On the red side, its montepulcianos, sangioveses and especially its tempranillo-based wines have performed very well indeed.

Visitor tips

A particularly rewarding winery in which to seek wine club membership, Wedding Oak is also an ideal stop for wine tourists driving from north or west Texas to the Hill Country.

McHenry is proud to consider Wedding Oak a catalyst in the gradual renaissance the town of San Saba is experiencing. When Wedding Oak was conceived, the area's main draws besides hunting and fishing were pecan products and Harry's Boots, a 1939-vintage emporium that had become a sprawling Western-wear megastore.

Harry's is still a draw — having expanded into a third of an acre of ranch and hunting wear — and San Saba's tiny downtown has seen the opening of several new boutiquish businesses while still maintaining its authentic feel. The Dofflemyer Hotel offers six rustic-chic rooms, and a remodeled San Saba Hotel is in the works. Wedding Oak visitors can stroll down the street from Wedding Oak to Old Man Scary Cellars, the Olive Oil Co. and Alamo Pecan (those nuts go well with Wedding Oak's Tioja, by the way).

Miles of river trails lead strollers from the historic Mill Pond Park to the LCRA San Saba River Nature Park and the older Risien Park. Area attractions include Gorman Falls at Colorado Bend State Park; two venerable suspension bridges; and, of course, the winery's namesake Wedding Oak.

WILLIAM CHRIS VINEYARDS

10352 U.S. 290, Hye. williamchriswines.com. Contact: 830-998-7654, info@williamchriswines.com. Tasting room open 10a-5p Mon-Wed, 10a-6p Thu-Sat, noon-5p Sun. Tasting fee; reservations recommended Mon-Thu, required Fri-Sun.

Brendon West for William Chris Vineyards

William Chris draws such crowds to the little town of Hye that reservations are recommended — especially if you want to get in on weekends.

Overview

There is no problem finding William Chris Vineyards. Had it not been for William Chris, Hye would be little more than a sign on the road instead of a fledgling wine hub on the "Wine Road 290."

Now, William Chris stops the traffic on U.S. 290 on Saturdays as Hill Country wine tourists flock there for the tasting and the live music. These days, you'll need to make a reservation if you want to make sure of getting in on the tasting.

The tasting-room patio overlooks seven acres of grapes (malbec, mourvèdre, tannat, merlot and petit verdot), and tables dotted around the live-oak-shaded grounds make this winery a great spot for picnics.

William Chris is among the first of the later generation of Texas wineries, having been founded in 2008. Bill Blackmon and Chris Brundrett combined their first names rather than their last because "they liked the sound." They had grown grapes and made wine in Texas for others, and now they decided it was time to do it for themselves.

They restored a 1905 farmhouse on the property to use as a tasting room; despite its diminutive size, it offered plenty of space at first, as their initial vintage was only eight barrels. The winery grew quickly, though, and a new tasting room was added in 2012.

Recognition also was quickly forthcoming for their wines, which were picked up by restaurants and cited in the media.

Philosophy

William Chris is a poster child for the modern focus on authenticity and transparency. From the beginning, the winery has never made a wine that did not use 100 percent Texas grapes. It sources from its own vineyard and from some 18 other growers in the Hill Country and High Plains. In 2017, the winery was a founding member of Texas Wine Growers, a group committed to using 100 percent Texas grapes.

Significant accomplishments

Blackmon and Brundrett have been in the front line of the ongoing legislative effort to redefine the "Texas" appellation on wine

A harvest scene at the William Chris estate vineyard.

labels to require 100 percent Texas grapes rather than the federally mandated level of at least 75 percent. The change would bring Texas into line with the three West Coast winemaking states of California, Oregon and Washington.

The duo also displays an innovative streak: In a state where a decent sparkling wine is mostly an unlikely dream, they make a rosé pétillant-naturel (frequently abbreviated to pét-nat), a sparkling wine made by bottling a still wine before fermentation is complete, leaving the remaining fermentation to finish in the bottle, producing effervescence.

Best wines

William Chris' mourvèdre is putting the grape on the state's map. California wine educator Clark Smith has said it "exemplifies rose aromas and feminine delicacy unique to Texas mourvèdre."

Visitor tips

Reservations are a must if you're visiting on a weekend, and a good idea even on weekdays. If you're in the neighborhood and thinking about dropping by, at least call first to check whether the tasting room can accommodate you.

Once there, you can choose to sit under the covered pavilion, on the deck or at a picnic table under sheltering oaks. Plates of cheeses from Austin's fine-cheese shop Antonelli's can be purchased; outdoor heaters and blankets are provided for chilly evenings, as well as bottled water and fans for the steamier days. Yes, you can bring your pooch, but check the rules on the website first. Troubadours serenade the crowd every Friday, Saturday and Sunday. Should you want something heftier than a cheese plate, or need a spot to wait out the crowds, head across the street to Hye Market, in Hye's former general store and post office.

William Chris' "Hye Society" wine club, so popular there's a waiting list, offers perks like admission to the Hye Society Lounge.

ABOUT THE AUTHOR

Andrew Chalk is a Dallas-based freelance writer and blogger who writes about wine, spirits, beer, food, restaurants, wineries and destinations all over the world. His articles have appeared in *The Daily Meal, John Mariani's Virtual Gourmet, Somm Journal, Wine-Searcher.com, Palate Press, Modern Lifestyles, The Dallas Morning News, D Magazine, Texas Wine & Trail Magazine* and *Food and Beverage Magazine.*

Based in Dallas, he holds the WSET Level 3 certification in wines and spirits, the Certified Specialist of Wine certification from the Society of Wine Educators and the Italian Wine Professional certification. He is a 2016 recipient of an open fellowship to the Symposium for Professional Wine Writers.

He has judged at the San Antonio Stock Show & Rodeo Wine Competition and the Houston Livestock Show and Rodeo International Wine Competition.

When not writing, he can usually be found participating in his favorite sport of soccer. He also likes cooking, at which he is lousy but enthusiastic.